The Individual in History

Gandhi

John Simkin

D1344963

Spartacus

Gandhi

ISBN 0 948865 86 5

Printed by Delta Press, Hove

Acknowledgements

Extracts: C. Allen, *Plain Tales from the Raj,* Andre Deutsch, (1975); D. Das, *India,* Collins, (1969); L. Fischer, *The Essential Gandhi,* Mentor, (1954); R.C. Majumdar, *'India's Struggle for Freedom,* Bharatiya, (1961); J. Nehru, *Toward Freedom,* Bodley Head, (1939); S. Bose, *The Indian Struggle,* Wishart, (1935) Gandhi, *Hind Swarf,* Navajivan, (1909); Gandhi, *An Autobiography,* Navajivan, (1927); R. Payne, *The Life and Death of Mahatma Gandhi,* Bodley Head, (1969); T. Heathcote, *The Indian Army,* David & Charles, (1974); G. Ashe, *Gandhi,* Stein & Day, (1968); B. Ambedkar, *What Congress and Gandhi have done to the Untouchables,* Thacker, (1946); W. Brown, *The United States and India,* Harvard, (1953); H. Alexander, *Gandhi Through Western Eyes,* Asia, (1969); R. Majumdar, *History of the Freedom Movement,* Bharatiya, (1963); P. Dutt, *India Today,* Bombay, (1949); A. Copley, *Gandhi,* Basil Blackwell, (1987); M. Edwardes, *The Last Years of British India,* Cassell, (1963); W. Golant, *The Long Afternoon,* Purnell, (1974); A.J.P. Taylor, *English History 1914-1945,* (1965); D. Sarma, *The Father of the Nation,* Madras, (1956); P. Mason, *A Matter of Honour,* Purnell, (1974); S. Ashton, *Indian Independence,* Batsford, (1985); S. Sarwar Hassan, *The Genesis of Pakistan,* Karachi, (1950); T. Unnithan, *Gandhi Free India,* Groningen, (1956); P. Moon, *Divide and Out,* Chatto and Windus, (1961); J. Sunderland, *India in Bondage,* Lewis Copland, (1960); S. Gopal, *Modern India,* Historical Association, (1967);

Illustrations: Punch Magazine: p63, p65, p79, The Times: p72 Bildarchiv Preussischer Kulturbesitz: p76 London Evening Standard: p82; Gandhi National Museum: p14, p17, p29, p40, p46, p50, p52 p54 p57; BBC Hulton Picture Library: p43, p47, p51(r); Sumati Mararjee Collection: p11, p21, p25: India Office Library: p45; Durban Local History Museum: p32.

The author would also like to thank Judith Simkin, Julia McGirr, David Simkin, Peter Mansbridge and John Gibney for their help in the production of this book.

Contents

Source Material

Introduction

Since his assassination in 1947, Gandhi has become one of the most loved and respected political leaders of all time. Louis Fischer, one of his biographers, claims that he is the greatest figure to emerge since Jesus Christ. The scientist, Albert Einstein, who was not known to exaggerate and had a considerable reputation for seeking the truth, commented after Gandhi's death: "Generations to come, it may be, will scarce believe that such a one as this ever in flesh and blood walked this earth."

It is difficult to imagine any other political leader in the 20th Century being described in this way. One reason for this is that Gandhi was a spiritual as well as political leader. Some of his supporters have compared him to the founders of the great world religions, such as Buddha, Mohammed, and Jesus Christ.

The status of Gandhi was also enhanced by the release in 1982 of the extremely popular feature film on his life. The millions who saw 'Gandhi' were no doubt influenced by the film-makers' sympathetic interpretation of Gandhi's personality and political career.

The main reason why Gandhi is so highly respected is that he was a man of peace. The 20th Century has been an extremely destructive period in world history and Gandhi was one of the few leaders of the dispossessed to have constantly advocated the use of non-violent action to solve political problems.

Many people believe that Gandhi's message is more relevant today than it has ever been. As S. Radhakristan of the 'Gandhi Peace Foundation' has pointed out: "His is the voice of the age to come, and not that which is fading and should fade away. We are at the crossroads of history. Man's greatest enemy is not disease or famine or demographic explosion, but nuclear weapons which in a war may completely destroy civilisation and in peace inflict grievous and lasting damage on the human race... Gandhi is the immortal symbol of love and understanding in the world wild with hatred and torn by misunderstanding."

It is because Gandhi has become a symbol of hope that historians have been reluctant to criticise him. However, one of the objectives of 'The Individual in History' is to encourage students to develop their own views on the figure being studied. Therefore this book contains comments by people who are highly critical of Gandhi's political ideas and achievements as well as those, who like Fischer, believe that he is the greatest political figure in the 20th Century.

For all the praise that has been showered on him since his death, it is interesting to note that Gandhi was extremely dissatisfied with his achievements. Just before his death he remarked: "(why) do congratulations come in? It will be more appropriate to say condolences. There is nothing but anguish in my heart."

For most of his life Gandhi had been campaigning for an end to Britain's control over India by peaceful methods. In 1947 India was granted its freedom but in the process over a million people were to lose their lives in the days that preceded and followed the granting of independence.

Gandhi was also depressed by other developments that were taking place in India. He was a strong supporter of traditional values and had a particular dislike of industrialisation and modern medicine. The strength with which he held these views is reflected in his decision in 1944 not to grant permission for his wife to be given the drug penicillin by her doctors, a decision which he knew might result in her death.

Gandhi also become despondent about the military developments that took place during the Second World War. Gandhi's belief in using non-violence to obtain political objectives was based on the idea that love could conquer hatred. He claimed that: "The unexpected spectacle of endless rows of men and women simply dying rather than surrender to the will of an aggressor must ultimately melt him and his soldiery." Gandhi's belief relied on the suffering of those employing 'passive-resistance' affecting the conscience of those bearing arms. For this to happen there had to be contact between the aggressor and the oppressed. Aerial warfare ensured that this did not take place. When asked by a reporter a few hours before he was assassinated how he would react to the dropping of an atom bomb on India, Gandhi replied: "I would come out in the open and let the pilot see I have not a trace of ill-will against him. The pilot will not see our faces from his great height, I know. But the longing in our hearts - that he will not come to harm - would reach up to him and his eyes would be opened. If those thousands who were done to death in Hiroshima, if they had died with that prayerful action... their sacrifice would not have gone in vain."

Many would see this statement as the words of an old man who had failed to come to terms with the modern world. Others would argue that the world's only hope for survival is to adopt Gandhi's belief that only love can conquer violence. Whatever your final judgement may be, I hope you agree that his actions as well as his opinions are well worth considering.

Childhood

Mohandas Gandhi was born at Porbandar, India, on 2nd October, 1869. Porbandar was part of Kathiawad, a small state ruled by several Indian princes.

Gandhi came from a fairly prosperous family. His father, Karamchand Gandhi, was the dewan or Prime Minister of Kathiawad. Karamchand had been married four times. His first two wives died and when he discovered that his third wife was suffering from an incurable disease, he decided to get married again. Karamchand, who was now over forty, was determined to find a wife who would enable him to have a large family. His chosen bride, Putlibai, was only thirteen and within a few years provided her husband with four children. The last child born was Mohandas who was later to become one of the most important figures in the 20th Century.

Mohandas did not see much of his elderly father who was kept busy administrating the state of Kathiawad. The main influence on Mohandas was his mother. Putlibai Gandhi was a deeply religious woman. She was a member of the Pranami sect, which combined elements of Hinduism and Mohammedanism. If you were a member of this sect you were not allowed to consume meat, alcohol or take any form of drug. The Pranami sect also believed in the importance of fasting. In his autobiography, Gandhi recalled how during one rainy season, his mother vowed not to eat food until the sun showed itself again: "We children on those days would stand, staring at the sky, waiting to announce the appearance of the sun to our mother. Everyone knows that at the height of the rainy season the sun often does not condescend to show his face. And I remember days when, at his sudden appearance, we would rush and announce it to her. She would run out to see with her own eyes, but by this time the fugitive sun would be gone, thus depriving her of her meal. 'That does not matter', she would say cheerfully, 'God did not want me to eat today.' And then she would return to her round of duties."

As a young boy Gandhi tried very hard to match his mother's dedication to the Pranami religion. However, there were times when he failed to resist temptation. This was not helped by the development of a friendship with a Muslim boy called Sheikh Mehtab. Gandhi's friend was everything that he was not. Whereas Gandhi was small, thin, unco-ordinated and shy, Sheikh was confident, outgoing, tall and a superb athlete. Gandhi idolised this boy who was three years his senior and when Sheikh Mehtab told him he owed his strength to meat-eating, Gandhi decided to change his diet.

Gandhi knew that his mother would be deeply upset if she

discovered her son had eaten meat so he insisted that they found a secret hiding place some distance from home to eat their meal. Later Gandhi wrote about his feelings concerning this meal: "I saw for the first time in my life - meat. There was baker's bread also. I relished neither. The goat's meat was as tough as leather. I simply could not eat it. I was sick and had to leave off eating. I had a bad night afterwards. A horrible nightmare haunted me. Every time I dropped off to sleep it would seem as though a live goat were bleating inside me, and I would jump up full of remorse."

Gandhi continued eating meat for over a year. However, he was never able to overcome his feelings of guilt. Desperate as he was to grow physically like his friend Sheikh Mehtab, he eventually decided that he could not carry on lying to his parents and he stopped.

Sheikh Mehtab also introduced Gandhi to smoking tobacco. To obtain money for this habit he began stealing money from his parents' servants. Gandhi was now very much under the influence of the older boy and when a friend of Sheikh Mehtab fell into debt, he agreed to sell a piece of stolen gold for them.

After he had completed the transaction, Gandhi was once again overcome by guilt. He decided to confess his sins in a letter to his father. Gandhi expected his father to punish him but instead he just sat and quietly cried. This increased his feelings of guilt even more and at that moment he vowed he would never steal, smoke tobacco or eat meat again. It was a vow he was to keep for the rest of his life.

At the age of thirteen, Gandhi married a girl called Kasturbhai Makaryi. Kasturbhai was Gandhi's father's third choice. The previous two girls had died before the marriage could take place. It was the custom in India for parents to arrange child marriages. Gandhi was later to criticise this practice but at the time, like all other young people in India, he accepted his new wife without complaint.

Gandhi was worried about how Kasturbhai would react to him. He was ashamed of his puny body and lack of courage. For example, Gandhi was extremely frightened of snakes and insisted that the light should be left on at night when he went to bed. Before his wedding, he worried endlessly about how his wife would react when she discovered that her husband was too scared to go to bed in the dark.

On the day of the wedding, Gandhi's father, Karamchand, was working away from home. In an attempt to make sure he arrived in time for the ceremony, he ordered the driver of the stagecoach to go as fast as he could. Just before the coach reached its destination, it was involved in an accident. Karamchand was seriously hurt in the crash. He never fully recovered from his injuries and died three

Gandhi at the age of seventeen

years later.

Although now a married man Gandhi continued to go to school. Gandhi was not an outstanding pupil. One of the main reasons for this was his poor attendance record. It was especially bad in the year following his marriage to Kasturbhai. Of the 222 school days in 1882, he attended on only 74 occasions. Gandhi was later to write that his marriage severely interrupted his studies and was one of the reasons why he became such a strong opponent of child marriages.

When Gandhi arrived at High School he discovered that most of his lessons were in English. Although he eventually mastered the language he found it greatly slowed down his rate of learning. He was further handicapped by the fact that most of the Indians who taught these subjects also had a poor grasp of the English language.

Studying subjects in English was Gandhi's first encounter with the way that India was dominated by Britain. At the time, Gandhi could not understand why his teachers insisted on using a foreign language to teach their subjects. It was by studying history that Gandhi was to find the answer to this question.

British Rule in India

British and other European merchants had been trading with India for hundreds of years. In 1600, the East India Company was formed. Its aim was to sell Indian products such as cotton, silk and sugar to world markets. The East India Company became very successful and by 1756 they were strong enough to raise an army under the leadership of Robert Clive to remove French traders from the area.

To guarantee control of Indian trade, the East India Company became increasingly involved in the internal government of the country. The Company built forts and recruited Indians to join their army. This army was used to maintain friendly and sympathetic Indian princes in power.

In 1857, soldiers of the East India Company rebelled. The main cause of the rebellion was a belief that the British were trying to force Hindus and Muslims to adopt Christian values and customs. This uprising gave the British government the excuse they needed to take over the control of the country from the East India Company.

In Britain, a Secretary of State for India was appointed. He in turn, appointed a Viceroy who was based in Delhi. The Viceroy served for a four year period and had the power to determine internal reforms and foreign policy. His high status is reflected by the fact that he was given 700 servants and was paid twice the salary of the British Prime Minister. By 1890, the Viceroy had approximately 1,000 British officials to help him rule a country of some 280 million Indians.

Gandhi in England

As Gandhi's home in Porbandar was some distance from the nearest large town, he saw very few white men as a child. However, he heard stories about how powerful they were. One of the ways that his friend Sheikh Mehtab had persuaded him to eat meat was by quoting to him a poem written by Narmad:

> Behold the mighty Englishman
> He rules the Indian small,
> Because being a meat-eater
> He is five cubits tall.

While in High School, Gandhi learnt a great deal about England. Although originally resentful at having to use a foreign language in his studies, Gandhi developed a strong desire to visit the 'mother' country. Mavji Dave, a Brahmin priest and close friend, suggested that when Gandhi finished High School, he should go to study for a law degree in London.

At first his family was opposed to the idea. The death of Karamchand had considerably reduced the family income and there was not enough money to pay for Gandhi's fare and course fees. Gandhi's mother was also concerned about him living in England. She had heard stories of how young Indians had abandoned their religious faith when studying there and had drunk wine, eaten meat and became involved with local girls. Gandhi vowed he would "not touch any of these things". Eventually he managed to convince her to let him go, but he still had the problem of raising the necessary funds. Laxmidas, Gandhi's elder brother and the person in charge of the family funds, decided the only way the money could be raised was by selling some of the family property. Kasturbhai, Gandhi's wife, also agreed to sell a portion of her jewellery.

Just before Gandhi was due to sail for England, members of the religious sect that he belonged to objected to his visit. Gandhi had to appear before a court of religious leaders and although he explained in great detail why he needed to study in England, they rejected his pleas. When Gandhi refused to obey their commands, he was told that in future he would be considered an 'outcaste'. They also threatened to punish any other member of the sect who helped Gandhi in his attempts to visit England. Although his family were deeply religious, they did not abandon him and the arrangements for his journey went ahead.

Gandhi's main problem in London was food. At that time, very few people in Britain were vegetarians and Gandhi was constantly being put under pressure to eat meat. His friends feared for his health but when they attempted to persuade him to eat meat, he would always reply: "A vow is a vow, it cannot be broken."

One night, while walking the streets of London, Gandhi came across a vegetarian restaurant. The restaurant also sold books on the subject. From these books Gandhi discovered the different reasons why people were vegetarians. He was particularly impressed by a book by Howard Williams called 'The Ethics of Diet'. It was at this point that, according to Gandhi, he became a vegetarian by choice rather than for religious reasons. Gandhi decided to join the London Vegetarian Society. He was soon being asked to make speeches on the subject. Gandhi was shy at first but these occasions gave him valuable experience at public speaking and this was to prove extremely useful in developing the skills needed to be a political leader.

While in London, Gandhi spent a considerable amount of time reading newspapers. As well as improving his English, they also

Kasturbhai Gandhi

provided him with information on politics. While he was in London, the main political issue was the debate for Home Rule for Ireland. Gandhi studied the arguments put forward for the Irish people to govern themselves. Gandhi hoped that one day he could make use of this information to help India gain its independence from Britain.

South Africa

When Gandhi arrived back in India after successfully completing his studies in London, the first news he received was that his mother had died a few months earlier. His brother, Laxmidas, had not told him before as he wanted to spare him this "blow in a foreign land."

Gandhi became a lawyer in Bombay. His first court case was a disaster. When it was time to interrogate the first witness, Gandhi could not think of any questions to ask. He immediately withdrew from the case and returned the fee to his client. Gandhi's confidence was shattered and he decided that he would not take up any more cases until, in his words, he had "the courage to conduct them."

Laxmidas, who was also a lawyer, provided him with some fairly routine legal work. Gandhi was not really happy doing this and in 1893, when he was offered a job in Pretoria, South Africa, he decided to take it. Gandhi was told that the job would last a year and involved helping in a very important lawsuit.

There was a large Indian community living in South Africa. This dated back to the middle of the nineteenth century when there was a need for unskilled workers in South Africa. Britain, which controlled both countries, arranged for large numbers of poor, unemployed Indians to go to work in South Africa's mines, mills and factories. These Indians became known as 'coolies' (manual labourers).

When Gandhi arrived in South Africa, he had to take a long overland journey to Pretoria. His employer had bought him a first-class ticket but when he reached Maritzburg, he was ordered out of his compartment by a railway official. When he refused to move the local police were called. When they arrived, they explained that in South Africa black people were not allowed to travel in first-class compartments.

Gandhi was furious at this blatant example of racial prejudice and decided to travel the rest of the way to Pretoria by stage-coach. However, when he tried to take his seat in the stage-coach, Gandhi was told that blacks were not allowed to mix with white passengers and he would have to sit with the black driver on top of the coach.

Gandhi's first instinct was to return to India: "I began to think of my duty. Should I fight for my rights or go back to India, or should I go to Pretoria without minding the insults, and return to India after finishing the case? It would be cowardice to run back to India without fulfilling my obligations. The hardships to which I was subjected were superficial - only a symptom of the deep disease of colour prejudice. I should try, if possible to root out the disease and suffer hardships in the process."

As soon as he arrived in Pretoria, Gandhi began to campaign against the way the whites in South Africa treated the Indian community. He wrote letters to newspapers, made speeches at meetings and tried to convince anyone who would listen that the Indians in South Africa should be treated with respect.

Dada Abdulla, a rich merchant who Gandhi had been sent to work for in South Africa, showed little interest in this campaign. Dada Abdulla was more concerned with winning his legal battle with another rich merchant called Tyeb Khan Mohammed. Gandhi could see that if the case proceeded, it would financially ruin both men. This was a serious issue as Muslim merchants regarded bankruptcy as dishonourable and many committed suicide when this happened to them.

Gandhi brought the two men together and persuaded them to agree to an out of court settlement. Dada Abdulla was extremely pleased with Gandhi as he received £37,000 plus all his court costs. To show his appreciation, Dada Abdulla gave Gandhi a lavish farewell party. At the party one of the guests showed Gandhi a copy of the 'Natal Mercury' newspaper. It contained a report that the South African State of Natal planned to remove the right of Indians to vote in elections. Gandhi was enraged and was soon lecturing the guests what would happen if the bill was passed. He urged them to organise against this attack on Indian civil rights. One of those listening suggested that he should stay and help plan the campaign. Dada Abdulla, who had by now been deeply influenced by Gandhi's views on human rights, agreed and volunteered to supply him with financial assistance.

In the weeks that were to follow, Gandhi made speeches, wrote letters, organised petitions and generally helped to build up opposition to the proposed bill. Gandhi also tried to use his contacts in London to help apply pressure on the Natal government. Dadabhai Naoroji, a former mathematics teacher from Bombay, but now Member of Parliament for Central Finsbury, was recruited into the campaign. Naoroji raised the issue in the House of Commons and set about gaining the support of politicians and other influential people in Britain.

As well as removing the vote from the Indian community, the Natal government was also proposing an annual tax of £25 on all Indian workers. This was more than most Indians earned in a year. It was clear that the intention of this measure was to force the

Gandhi as a barrister in South Africa

Indians to leave the country.

Gandhi realised that only a large, powerful organisation could stop these measures going through. He decided to form a Natal branch of the Indian National Congress, a group fighting for independence back in India.

With the support of influential people in Britain and India, Gandhi's organisation was able to reduce the £25 tax to £3. Some Indians were also allowed to keep the vote but the de-franchisement bill was still passed. Gandhi had been encouraged by the success of the campaign but overall felt defeated. He knew that there was no other option open to him, he must stay in South Africa and continue the fight for the Indian community.

The Green Book

In 1896, Gandhi returned to India to make arrangements for his family to join him in South Africa. While in his home country he took the opportunity to meet the leaders of the Indian National Congress. Gandhi gave a good impression and as a result of these meetings he was invited to make a speech to a large gathering of the movement in Bombay.

Gandhi had always been prone to bouts of nervousness when talking in front of a large audience. This happened once again in Bombay. As he was to recall later in his autobiography: "This was the first meeting of the kind in my experience. I saw that my voice could only reach a few. I was trembling as I began my speech. Sir Pherozeshah (the chairman of the meeting) cheered me up continually by asking me to speak louder and still louder. I have a feeling that, far from encouraging me, it made my voice sink lower and lower. My old friend Keshavrao Deshpande came to my rescue. I handed my speech to him."

Gandhi was upset that he was unable to finish the speech himself but he was delighted by the reception the audience gave him at the end. The members of the Indian National Congress had been shocked by the way the Indian community in South Africa was being treated and were grateful for the work that Gandhi was doing.

While in India Gandhi was encouraged to write about his experiences in South Africa. Gandhi agreed and this material was published in a pamphlet with the title, 'The Grievances of the British Indians in South Africa: An Appeal to the Indian Public'. As the title was so long, the pamphlet became known as the 'Green Book'.

The 'Green Book' was a great success and within weeks a second edition was being printed. Although this helped to establish Gandhi as an important figure in India, it made him extremely unpopular with the white population in South Africa. This became clear to him when he arrived back in South Africa. A right-wing political group called the 'Colonial Patriotic Union', whose policy it was to expel all Indians from Natal, organised a hostile reception for Gandhi at Durban harbour.

At first the Natal government refused permission for Gandhi to land. After being kept on board for 26 days it was eventually agreed that he could leave the boat. It was suggested by the police that Gandhi should adopt some form of disguise. This he refused to do and as soon as he left the protection of the boat, the crowd threw stones, bricks and rotten fish at him. When they got close enough they hit him with sticks and whips. For a moment it looked like he would be beaten to death. His life was saved by Mrs Alexander, the wife of the police superintendent. Swinging her umbrella, she was able to force the crowd away from Gandhi until the police arrived from the local police station.

Gandhi was taken to a house of a friend who lived close by. However, within minutes, a large crowd assembled outside the house demanding that unless Gandhi came out, they would set fire to the building. There was only one solution left - he was forced to accept the original advice of wearing a disguise. Gandhi put on a police constable's uniform and, accompanied by a detective disguised as an Indian merchant, walked through the crowds of people who were demanding that he should be hanged from the nearest tree.

The Boer War

In South Africa there was not only conflict between the whites and the blacks. Some of the white settlers were farmers of Dutch descent called Boers. They resented the rule of the British and during the 1830s they set-up two independent areas called the Orange Free State and the Transvaal.

When gold was discovered in the Transvaal in 1886, British settlers began to move into Boer territory. These immigrants became known as Uitlanders. They were allowed into the Transvaal because their skills were needed but the hostility between the two groups remained and this was reflected in the decision by the Boers to refuse the Uitlanders the right to vote. The Uitlanders sent a petition to the British government explaining their complaints and requesting them to take action against the Boers. Negotiations took place but no satisfactory solution could be found and in 1899 fighting broke out between the two sides.

Gandhi had mixed feelings about the Boer War. He disliked the idea of people being killed but he saw the war as providing an opportunity for Indians to obtain civil rights in South Africa. Gandhi wrote later that : "If I demanded rights as a British citizen, it was also my duty, as such, to participate in the defence of the British Empire. I held then that India could achieve her complete emancipation only within and through the British Empire."

Gandhi was of the opinion that the: "average Englishman believed that the Indian was a coward, incapable of taking risks or looking beyond his immediate self-interest." Gandhi hoped that Indian participation in the war would convince the British government that they deserved equality with the whites in South Africa.

Gandhi went to see the British administration in South Africa and offered to recruit Indians for the war effort. The plan was initially rejected. A British official cruelly replied that: "Indians know nothing of war. You would only be a drag on the army. You would have to be taken care of instead of being a help to us."

The success of the Boers in the early stages of the war and an acute manpower shortage resulted in a change of mind and Gandhi was given the go ahead to form an Ambulance Corps. However, it was stipulated that they could only act as stretcher-bearers and must not get too close to the fighting."

It did not take Gandhi long to recruit 1,100 Indians into his Ambulance Corps. During the next few weeks they were to provide a valuable service to the hard pressed British troops. The stipulation that the Indians were not to enter the battlefield was soon forgotten as they were called up to carry the wounded back to the safety of British held territory.

The relationship that was to develop between the Indian Ambulance Corps and the British soldiers had a deep impact on Gandhi. He recalled one incident when the British were retreating from the advancing Boer forces: "Everyone was thirsting for water. There was a tiny brook on the way where we could slake our thirst. But who was to drink first? We had proposed to come in after the tommies (British soldiers) had finished. But they would not begin first and urged us to do so, and for a while a pleasant competition went on for giving precedence to one another."

These experiences taught Gandhi that it was possible for whites to treat Indians as equals. However, this did not last long for after six weeks it was decided to disband the Indian Ambulance Corps. The Indian community was not rewarded with any change to civil rights legislation, although thirty-eight members of the Indian Ambulance Corps, including Gandhi, were awarded the 'Boer War Medal'.

In the months that followed, Gandhi continued to campaign for Britain and helped to raise considerable amounts of money for the war effort. Gandhi's loyalty to the British Empire is reflected in the telegram that he sent to the British government on the death of Queen Victoria in 1901. It read: "British Indians in Natal tender humble condolences to the Royal Family in their bereavement and join Her Majesty's other children in bewailing the Empire's loss in the death of the greatest and most loved Sovereign on earth."

Later that year, Gandhi decided to return to India with his wife and four sons. As an acknowledgement of the work that he had done for the Indian community, the Gandhi family were given gifts worth approximately one thousand pounds. The most valuable item was a gold necklace given to Gandhi's wife, Kasturbhai. However, Gandhi told her that he had decided to give all the gifts to the Natal Indian Congress. He was supported in this by his two eldest sons, Harilal and Manilal.

Gandhi in South Africa

Kasturbhai was furious. In the past she had sold her jewellery in order to help pay for her husband's education. Now she was being asked to give away something that she desperately wanted to own. From the argument that took place it became clear that there was a clash of values. For sometime Gandhi had been attempting to simplify his life. He had removed all costly ornaments from his home. He disapproved of money being spent on expensive clothes. Gandhi believed that all spare money should go to the Natal Indian Congress. He argued that it was only through this organisation that the Indian community would ever obtain justice.

When Gandhi claimed that the necklace had been given to Kasturbhai only because of the service he had given to the community, she replied: "But service rendered by you is as good as rendered by me. I have toiled for you day and night. Is that no service?"

Kasturbhai then went on to complain how she had been forced to wait on beggars and lepers whom Gandhi invited into their home. Although she supported Gandhi's belief that they should serve the poor, it was often her, the woman of the house, who had the job of looking after them.

Gandhi admitted that: "these were pointed thrusts, and some of them went home. But I was determined to return the ornaments... " Later Gandhi was to claim :"I have never since regretted the step, and as the years have gone by, my wife has also seen its wisdom. It has saved us from many temptations."

Brahmacharya

After travelling around India talking to senior members of the Indian National Congress, Gandhi settled down to practise law in Bombay. It was at this time that he became interested in health-care. The reason for this was that his ten year old son, Manilal, had a severe attack of typhoid. Soon afterwards he also developed pneumonia. A doctor was called and his advice was that Manilal should adopt a diet of eggs and chicken broth. Gandhi replied that: "rightly or wrongly it is part of my religious conviction that man may not eat meat, eggs and the like. Even for life itself we may not do certain things." With the warning that Manilal would probably die without the prescribed treatment, Gandhi decided to treat the boy himself. To reduce his son's fever, Gandhi wrapped him in wet sheets. Although Manilal disliked this treatment, Gandhi managed to persuade him to continue until his temperature fell. For the next forty days the boy was put on a diet of diluted milk and fruit juice.

The boy recovered and Gandhi became convinced that his unusual methods of dealing with illness worked. Others shared his conviction and for the rest of his life people asked him how to cure their medical problems. The remedies that Gandhi suggested were invariably a combination of prayer, diet and careful nursing.

When the Boer War ended in 1902, Gandhi went back to South Africa with the hope that he could persuade the victorious British to reward the Indian community who had so loyally supported the Empire. Gandhi was to discover that Joseph Chamberlain, the Secretary of State for the Colonies, was more concerned with improving the relationship between the two groups of white settlers in South Africa. Gandhi was particularly upset to find out that the

British government was compensating the Boers for the damage caused by the war. To Gandhi, the idea of paying money to the 'enemy' while ignoring the political claims of the loyal Indians was extremely unfair.

Disillusioned by these events, Gandhi concentrated on his work as a lawyer. As he was very popular with the Indian merchants he soon built up a successful law practice in Johannesburg.

Gandhi never lost his interest in politics and in an attempt to spread his ideas he formed his own newspaper called the 'Indian Opinion'. The newspaper lost money but Gandhi was able to subsidise it from the profits that he made from his law practice.

In 1906 war broke out between the Zulus, an African tribe from Natal, and the white South Africans. Gandhi admitted that he "bore no grudge against the Zulus" as "they had harmed no Indian". In fact he was sympathetic to the Zulus' decision not to pay a new tax imposed by the Government that had caused the conflict. However, he believed that this war, like the Boer War, provided an opportunity for Indians to show their loyalty to the Empire. In a series of articles that he wrote for the 'Indian Opinion', Gandhi encouraged the Indian community to join the voluntary forces to put down the Zulu rebellion.

Opponents of Gandhi criticised his stance on this issue. They argued that it was morally unacceptable to encourage others to kill another oppressed group in order to prove their patriotism.

Once again, Gandhi was unable to persuade the South African government to allow the Indians to join the army. As with the Boer War, Gandhi formed an Ambulance Corps.

The war soon petered out and Sergeant Major Gandhi and his men spent most of their time treating captured Zulus who had been flogged by the South African army.

Gandhi often marched fifty miles a day during the war. In his autobiography he reveals that this time was often spent in deep thought. He came to the conclusion that family life had interfered with his duty to the community. Although only 36, Gandhi decided that he would no longer live the life of a married man: "On the present occasion, for instance," he argued, "I should not have been able to throw myself into the fray, had my wife been expecting a baby."

It was while he was in the Ambulance Corps that Gandhi took his vow of chastity, or what he called 'brahmacharya'. In doing so, he decided to devote himself completely to the community rather than his family.

Brahmacharya was to become an important part of Gandhi's political philosophy: "Life without brahmacharya appears to me to be insipid and animal like. Man is man because he is capable of, and only in so far as he exercises self-restraint."

Gandhi saw within man a struggle between body and spirit. It was the endless desires of the body that were the causes of many of the world's problems. "By means of the body we practise a thousand things which we would do better to avoid: cunning, self-indulgence, deceit, stealing, adultery etc." By adopting a vow of chastity and going on regular fasts, Gandhi was attempting to restrain his bodily desires. If successful, Gandhi believed God, rather than Satan, would take control of both his body and spirit.

Asiatic Law Amendment

On August 22, 1906, the Transvaal government announced the decision to pass the 'Asiatic Law Amendment' Act. This law stated that all Indians over the age of eight must be fingerprinted and carry with them at all times a certificate of registration. If any Indians were found without a certificate, the Transvaal government would have the power to fine, imprison or deport them.

Gandhi realised that this law would severely restrict the freedom of the Indian community. He especially objected to the idea of being fingerprinted. Gandhi knew that normally only criminals were forced to have their fingerprints taken.

A public meeting was arranged in Johannesburg. Three thousand of the thirteen thousand Indians living in the Transvaal turned up to hear Gandhi speak. Gandhi told the meeting that he was willing to make a vow that he would always refuse to be fingerprinted or to carry around the required registration documents. He urged the people at the meeting to follow his example.

Gandhi also explained his policy of 'ahimsa'. Gandhi argued that if employed by large enough numbers, 'passive resistance' against the law, would force the government to back down. Gandhi warned the audience that such a strategy would involve a great deal of suffering: We may have to go to jail, where we may be insulted. We may have to go hungry and suffer extreme heat... we may be flogged.... we may be deported... In short, therefore, it is not at all impossible that we may have to endure every hardship that we can imagine, and wisdom lies in pledging ourselves on the understanding that we shall have to suffer all that and worse."

Observers at the meeting claimed later that everyone present agreed to follow Gandhi and vow not to be fingerprinted or to carry registration documents. To celebrate the occasion they all sung 'God Save the King'.

Gandhi employed 'Indian Opinion' in his campaign against the 'Asiatic Law Amendment'. In one article, where he explained the strategy of passive resistance, he asked readers to send in a name to

Gandhi with two of his British supporters,
Charlie Andrews and William Pearson.

describe this policy. The name he selected was 'Satyagraha', which
means "truth-force". From now on, Gandhi's followers would be
called 'satyagrahi'.

In October, 1906, Gandhi went to London in an attempt to
persuade the British government to overrule the Transvaal
authorities. They were generally sympathetic but Winston Churchill,
the Under Secretary of State for the Colonies, warned Gandhi that
when the Transvaal gained self-government, they would be able to
do as they pleased.

On his way back to South Africa by boat, Gandhi received a telegram informing him that the British government had decided to refuse permission for the 'Asiatic Law Amendment' to come into operation. The success of Gandhi's campaign turned him into the most important Indian leader in the Transvaal. Wherever he went, he was greeted by cheering crowds. However, the celebrations did not last long. In January, 1907, the Transvaal was granted self-government. One of the first acts of the new administration was to introduce a law that stated that all Indians had to be registered and fingerprinted.

Gandhi knew that his campaign against this law would only be successful if the vast majority of Indians did not register. In an attempt to apply pressure on those who were unsure what to do, pickets were instructed to wait outside registration offices. Efforts were made to persuade these Indians not to register. If they did, the pickets took their names and they were later printed in 'Indian Opinion' under the heading 'Blacklegs'.

This tactic was successful and of the 13,000 Indians in the Transvaal, only 511 people registered. The police then started arresting those Indians who helped organise the campaign. The first was Ram Sundara who had made several speeches against Indians being fingerprinted. Ram Sundara was found guilty and sentenced to one month in prison. When he was released he was garlanded with flowers and paraded through the streets. However, his hero status was short-lived. Rather than return to prison by continuing to refuse to register, Ram Sundara decided to leave the Transvaal. Gandhi was furious as he had been deprived of a martyr. Gandhi's bitterness is reflected in an article that he wrote for 'Indian Opinion'. It included the passage: "As far as the community is concerned, Ram Sundara is dead as from today. He lives to no purpose. He has poisoned himself by his own hand. Physical death is to be preferred to such social death."

A few days after this article appeared, Gandhi himself was sentenced to two months imprisonment. It was the first of many spells spent in prison. Gandhi said he did not mind as it gave him plenty of opportunity to read books and think deeply about religion and politics.

While he was in prison, Gandhi had secret meetings with the Transvaal government. General Smuts, who was chosen to represent the government, offered to repeal the law if Gandhi promised to support voluntary registration. Gandhi saw this as a victory and signed the agreement.

Large sections of the Indian community were extremely annoyed with Gandhi's decision. Rumours were circulated that Gandhi had been paid £15,000 to call off the campaign. Several Indians threatened Gandhi that they would kill him for this betrayal.

Gandhi was convinced that he had done the right thing and decided that he would lead his followers to the registration offices. His opponents were equally determined to stop him and on the way to the offices he was attacked by a group of men. By the time the attackers had been chased off, Gandhi was lying unconscious in a pool of blood.

Gandhi decided to go ahead with his plan to register and arranged for government officials to visit him in hospital with the necessary documents. However, as the months passed, Gandhi gradually became aware that he had made a mistake in signing an agreement with the Transvaal government. Taking advantage of the split in the Indian community, the government made plans to introduce more restrictive laws against them.

By the summer of 1908, Gandhi was once more involved in the campaign against registration. A few months previously, Gandhi had told people to register, now he instructed them to burn their registration certificates. This resulted in his being arrested again. This time he was sentenced to two months hard labour. He was only out for a few weeks when he was convicted again. After serving three months, Gandhi decided to visit Britain to see if he could repeat the success of 1906.

Hind Swaraj

Gandhi stayed in London for several months. Once again he met with senior government ministers. Although they were sympathetic, they were unwilling to take action that would antagonise the white population in South Africa.

Independence for countries within the Empire was becoming an important issue at that time. India in particular was pressing very hard for some form of self-government. Some young Indian nationalists were willing to resort to violence to obtain their objectives. Just before Gandhi arrived in London, Madanlal Dhingra had murdered Sir Curzon Wyllie, a political adviser to the Secretary of State for India. In his trial, Dhingra claimed he had killed Sir Curzon Wyllie: "to avenge the crimes committed by the British in India."

Dhingra was a member of a terrorist organisation led by Shyamji Krishnavarma, the editor of the radical magazine, 'The Indian Sociologist'. Gandhi was concerned by the attraction for these terrorist groups to young Indians. On the long boat trip back to South Africa, Gandhi decided to write a book explaining why Indians should reject the use of violence in their attempts to gain independence from Britain. The book was called 'Hind Swaraj'

(Indian Home Rule) and was made up of a dialogue between a supporter of Indian terrorism and Gandhi. Gandhi later claimed that the book was based on interviews he had with terrorists while he was in London.

Gandhi also took the opportunity in the book to describe the kind of India he would like to see evolve after independence. Gandhi was opposed to the modernisation that had began to take place in India. He called for a return to the India of a thousand years ago, where farmers ploughed the fields using primitive equipment. He wrote that: "The railways, telegraphs, hospitals, lawyers, doctors and such like have all to go; and the so-called upper classes have to live consciously, religiously and deliberately the simple peasant life, knowing it to be a life giving me happiness."

Gandhi had been influenced by the ideas of Leo Tolstoy. Tolstoy, the famous Russian author of 'War and Peace' and 'Anna Karenina', had spent the last years of his life writing about political and social problems. Gandhi was particularly interested in Tolstoy's belief that political change could be obtained by 'passive resistance'. Tolstoy also believed that only the Russian peasants, living the simple life, were truly happy.

Gandhi acknowledged his debt to Tolstoy's teaching by describing himself as one of his disciples. In an attempt to spread these ideas, Gandhi published articles by Tolstoy in 'Indian Opinion'.

Tolstoy was nearing the end of his life when he first received contact from Gandhi. It pleased him that such an important political leader as Gandhi should be a follower of his ideas. Just before he died in 1910, Tolstoy wrote a long letter to Gandhi. In the letter he told Gandhi that: "your activity in the Transvaal... is the most essential work, the most important of all the work now being done in the world."

Tolstoy Farm

In May, 1910, Hermann Kallenbach, a wealthy German architect, gave Gandhi a 1,100 acres farm near Johannesburg. Gandhi saw this as his opportunity to build an 'ashram'. An ashram is a religious retreat whose members are bound together by a series of common vows. Gandhi called his ashram 'Tolstoy Farm'.

As well as his own family, Gandhi invited a wide variety of people to live with him. The ashram included Hindus, Muslims, Parsis and Christians. Gandhi hoped that he could create a society where people of different religions could live together in peace.

Gandhi encouraged these people to maintain their religious customs but he also expected them to follow his moral guidelines.

Gandhi at Tolstoy Farm

Members of the Tolstoy community were not allowed to eat meat or grain. Nor were they permitted to drink milk. Even roots like ginger were banned. Gandhi justified this by arguing: "that a joint of which proliferated into so many shoots, must indeed be full of lives. Moreover, to eat fresh shoots was as good as killing delicate babies."

With over 1,000 fruit trees on the farm, plenty of fertile land to grow vegetables and two wells, Tolstoy Farm was virtually self-sufficient.

Gandhi laid down strict rules of behaviour on the farm. All members of the community were required to work in the fields. All meals were taken together and everyone took it in turn to carry out the normal domestic chores.

Although the discipline was strict, Gandhi did not believe in corporal punishment. However, some of his rulings do appear to be fairly harsh. When, for example, he discovered that some of the boys had been making advances towards two Hindu girls, instead of punishing the boys, he ordered the girls to shave their heads to make them unattractive to the opposite sex.

Gandhi felt very strongly about the vow of chastity and when he discovered that two boys had broken this rule he became extremely angry. Gandhi told Kallenbach that as the leader of the community, he must punish himself for the boys' crime. Gandhi therefore decided he would fast for seven days.

Gandhi had learnt from his experiences as a child that guilt is an effective method of controlling people's behaviour. As he wrote later: "I felt that the only way the guilty parties could be made to realise my distress and the depth of their own fall would be for me to do some penance." This strategy reveals the deep, loving relationship that he had with his followers. As he himself pointed out: "Where there is no true love between the teacher and the pupil, when the pupil's delinquency has not touched the very being of the teacher and where the pupil has no respect for the teacher, fasting is out of place and may even be harmful."

One person Gandhi could not control was his eldest son, Harilal. Harilal was twenty-two when he came to live at Tolstoy Farm. There had been conflict between the two for some time. Harilal had married Gulab, a lawyer's daughter, against his father's advice. Gandhi had expected his son to follow his example and make a vow of chastity. This Harilal refused to do and Gulab went on to give birth to five children.

Harilal also objected to the authoritarian way that his father treated his mother. Another problem was Gandhi's refusal to allow Harilal to go to school. Gandhi believed that schools were a bad influence on young minds and when he found the time, attempted to teach his sons at home. Harilal suspected that the main reason his father wanted them educated at home was so that he would have more control over his sons.

Like his brothers, Harilal had always supported his father's political objectives and his actions had resulted in his serving several terms of imprisonment. However, he was determined to become a lawyer, and in 1911 he broke all ties with his father and left Tolstoy Farm for an education in India.

Newcastle Coal Strike

In March, 1913, the South African Supreme Court announced that all marriages that did not take place in a Christian church, were invalid. This meant that according to the government nearly all Indian children were illegitimate and could not inherit their parents' property.

Gandhi now had another government ruling to fight. It was decided to attempt to recruit the support of Indian workers. Gandhi and some of his followers marched to Newcastle, a town completely owned by local mineowners. Gandhi pleaded with the miners to come out on strike against the oppressive laws that the government was using against the Indian community. The miners knew that they were in danger of losing their homes as well as their jobs if they agreed to Gandhi's proposal. However, Gandhi's arguments were persuasive, and over 2,000 men came out on strike.

Gandhi's plan was to march the men to Tolstoy Farm where he promised he would supply them with food and shelter. On November 6, 1913, Gandhi led 2,037 men, 127 women and 57 children out of Newcastle. They were all instructed not to retaliate if attacked. Gandhi hoped, and expected, the protesters would be arrested. He did not have the resources to feed such a large group and doubted their ability to reach their destination of Tolstoy Farm.

The police decided not to arrest the marchers. Gandhi's problems of feeding his supporters increased as people from the towns they went through also joined the march. Rumours also began to spread that the reason why the police were holding back was that white farmers planned to open fire on the marchers.

Gandhi began to worry about the responsibility of leading such a march. If the farmers opened fire on the marchers, he would have caused their deaths by encouraging them to leave Newcastle. Gandhi sent a telegram to the South African government claiming that:"if deaths occur, especially among women with babies in arms, responsibility will be the government's."

In an attempt to stop the march, the police arrested Gandhi. Gandhi suspected that this would happen and had already made alternative arrangements for others to lead the march. When the police realised the march was continuing they released Gandhi. They were aware that with Gandhi in prison there was more chance that the marchers would resort to violence.

When the marchers reached Volksrust, the police tried another strategy. Gandhi was arrested and sentenced to nine months imprisonment. The rest of the marchers were then sent to prison. However, in order to get the men back to work, Newcastle coal mine was designated as a new prison. Mine officials were appointed as prison guards, and those who refused to work received severe beatings.

The Newcastle strike had ended in defeat for Gandhi but his new tactic of involving industrial workers worried the South African government. The country owed its wealth and prosperity to industrial production and strikes would pose a serious threat to this situation.

Gandhi (second from right) at the time of the Newcastle Coal Strike. On Gandhi's right is H. Kallenbach.

International pressure on the South African government was also increasing. Lord Hardinge, the Viceroy of India, claimed that the "passive resistance" movement had been "dealt with by measures which would not for one moment be tolerated by any country that called itself civilised." Other world figures made similar statements and eventually the South African government agreed to abolish the £3 tax on Indian workers. The 'Black Act' that invalidated non-Christian marriages was repealed and all Gandhi's followers were released from prison.

The Indian community saw this as a great victory. It had taken them eight years but the legislation introduced against Indians had finally been withdrawn. But Gandhi's Natal Indian Congress had only managed to return to the situation that existed before the campaign had started. The Indians had not been granted equality with the white community and were still treated as second-class citizens in South Africa.

Although aware of this, Gandhi came to the conclusion that it was a good time to leave South Africa. Laxmidas, his eldest brother, had recently died and Gandhi was now the head of the family. Under Indian custom, Gandhi was responsible for his brother's family. Gandhi had argued for several years that his first obligation was to the Indian community and not his family. However, there were far more Indians in India than South Africa, and with a large family to look after, he decided to go home. It was the last time that he would ever see South Africa and the Indians that he left behind him had good reason to find it a sad occasion. Seventy years later, the Indians are still waiting to achieve full civil rights in South Africa.

The First World War

Gopal Gokhale, the leader of the Indian Congress Party, suggested that Gandhi should travel with him to London before going back to India. Gokhale, who was very ill, hoped that Gandhi would take over the leadership of the party after his death. Although Gandhi was an experienced campaigner in South Africa, he knew little of Indian politics. Gokhale used the long boat trip to brief Gandhi on recent developments and advised him on how to behave when he arrived back in India.

Gandhi, Gokhale and Kallenbach reached London on August 6, 1914, just two days after Britain had declared war on Germany. Kallenbach, who was a German citizen, was immediately arrested and sent off to an internment camp. Gandhi appealed that his friend was a pacifist and posed no threat to the security of Britain, but the authorities were not impressed by his arguments and Kallenbach was not released.

As with the Boer War, Gandhi was keen to show that he was a loyal supporter of the British Empire. He wrote to the Under Secretary of State for India, offering his help in persuading the Indian community to help in the war effort.

Once again, Gandhi suspended his belief in 'ahimsa' while Britain was at war. Gandhi justified this change by the claim that Indians could improve their status by giving help and co-operation to Britain "in their hour of need". Gandhi was also of the opinion that while the war was going on, Indians should not press their demands for independence.

Some Indian nationalists took the view that with Britain in difficulty, it was in fact the best time to exert pressure on the government to grant self-rule. As one Indian remarked to Gandhi: "We are slaves and they are masters. How can a slave co-operate with the master in the hour of the latter's need?"

Gandhi rejected this argument: "I knew the difference of status between an Indian and an Englishman, but I did not believe that we had been quite reduced to slavery. I felt then that it was more the fault of individual British officials than of the British system, and that we could convert them by love." By supporting the British in "their hour of need", Gandhi hoped to increase the British people's affection for the Indian community. This love and affection,Gandhi believed, would eventually be expressed by a willingness to let India have its independence.

As on the previous two occasions when Gandhi offered help to Britain during a war, the British government suggested that he should form an 'Ambulance Corps'. This he agreed to do and within a few days he had recruited sixty Indians living in London to join the organisation.

In India itself, support for the British war effort was also strong. Over one million men were recruited into the army and over £100 million was raised to help pay for the war.

The Untouchables

Soon after arriving back in India, Gandhi set about building up a similar community to Tolstoy Farm in South Africa. With the help of some rich textile merchants, Gandhi set up an 'ashram' in Kochrab. The rules were like those imposed at Tolstoy Farm. All members had to make nine vows. These promises reflected Gandhi's strong opinions about celibacy, vegetarianism and tolerance to others. There was also a new vow introduced that was to cause considerable conflict within the community.

For some time Gandhi had questioned the caste system in India.

34

This was a system that divided all Hindus into four main groups. The Brahmins (priestly or learned class); Kshatriyas (the fighting class); Vaiskyas (traders) and Sudras (servants). Hindus believed that the four castes represented the four parts of the severed body of Purusha, the male form of their God, Brahma.

Hindus inherited their caste from their parents. Being a member of a caste severely restricted your behaviour. It controlled your occupation and the people with whom you had social contact ; for instance, you could not marry someone from outside your caste.

As well as the four main castes, there was also a fifth group called Harijans (untouchables). This group of 40 million people were completely excluded from having contact with the rest of society.

When Dudabhai, an untouchable, brought his family to Kochrab and asked to join the ashram, Gandhi agreed. Although the Kochrab community had made a vow to accept untouchables, their presence created a great stir. Even Gandhi's wife, Kasturbhai, threatened to leave the ashram if the Dudabhai family continued to live in Kochrab. Gandhi replied that he would be sorry to lose her but his belief that all Indians, regardless of caste, should mix freely together, came first. After Gandhi managed to convince the members of the ashram to accept the Dudabhai family, pressure began to be applied by outsiders. The ashram did not have its own water supply and a well outside its territory had to be used. The owner became very hostile when he discovered it was being used by an untouchable.

The rich merchants who originally supplied the money for Gandhi's ashram were also annoyed about the arrival of the untouchables and began to cut off funds. It seemed that the ashram would have to close but at the last moment, Ambalal Sarabhai, an owner of a big cloth mill, donated them 13,000 rupees, which was enough to keep it going for another year.

The Indigo Workers' Campaign

For over a hundred years, British firms based in Bengal had made large profits from the indigo plant. Local farmers preferred growing food crops and so a law was passed that forced them to put three-twentieths of their land aside for indigo. The peasants resented this as the price they received for their indigo was kept artificially low.

Just before the outbreak of the First World War profits from indigo dropped dramatically. The reason for this was the production of synthetic dyes in Europe. The Indian farmers were not aware of this and when it was suggested that the law forcing them to produce indigo would be repealed in exchange for higher rents they willingly agreed. Later, when they discovered they had been tricked, the peasants rioted. Armed guards soon put down the rebellion and the leaders of the riot were executed. In a stronger position than ever, the factory owners and landowners imposed a new tax on the peasants. This involved the peasant farmers paying money to the local factory owner when their sons and daughters got married. This was similar to the situation that existed in Medieval England.

The fighting in Europe during the First World War severely disrupted the production of synthetic dyes and the price of indigo increased rapidly. Once again the peasants were put under extreme pressure to grow indigo plants rather than food crops.

Raj Kumar Shukla, one of the indigo farmers from Bihari, decided to visit Lucknou, where the Indian National Congress was involved in an important meeting. Shukla approached several of the party leaders but they told him that they were too busy trying to obtain Indian independence to become involved in individual disputes. This was also Gandhi's view at first, but Shukla, who followed Gandhi around for days, eventually persuaded him to visit the village of Champarai.

When Gandhi saw the suffering of the peasants in Champarai he decided to set up an inquiry into the indigo trade. His first task was to recruit a team willing to record the testimonies of the peasant farmers. Several local lawyers and teachers volunteered to help. Before accepting their offer, Gandhi told them that while working for him they had to give up eating meat and employing servants. This they agreed to do and within a few weeks they had collected twenty-five thousand statements from the indigo farmers.

The factory owners applied pressure on the British authorities to arrest Gandhi. They refused to do this as they were aware that the imprisonment of Gandhi would create massive publicity which would eventually result in a national campaign for the reform of the indigo industry.

The Lieutenant Governor of Bihar agreed to set up his own commission to look into the exploitation of the indigo farmers and Gandhi became one of its members. After much discussion, the commission negotiated a 25% reduction in the rents of the indigo farmers.

Some of Gandhi's critics claimed that he should have persuaded the commission to behave more generously to the indigo farmers. Gandhi replied that he believed it would boost the peasants' confidence if they saw the landowners back down, and it would encourage them to defend their rights in the future. As he wrote later: "The main thing was to rid the farmers of their fear by making them realise that the officials were not the masters."

After the events of Bihar, Gandhi was seen as an expert on

industrial disputes. Appeals came from workers all over India asking him to help them in their disputes with their employers. Gandhi helped several groups but always insisted on certain conditions, the main one being that they would never resort to violence in their attempts to improve their pay and conditions. When, as happened in one case, workers started threatening 'blacklegs', Gandhi fasted until discipline was restored.

One of the strangest cases Gandhi was involved in took place in Ahmedabad. A young woman complained to Gandhi about the low wages that were being paid at a local cotton mill. The mill was owned by her brother, Ambalal Sarabhai. Sarabhai was also the same man who had given Gandhi 13,000 rupees to keep his ashram open. Gandhi was in a difficult position but eventually decided that the wages were indeed poor and he agreed to advise the workers in their dispute with Sarabhai. After three days, Sarabhai gave in and increased their wages.

Amritsar

By 1918, the tactics employed in the First World War had taken their toll and the British army was desperately short of troops. The Viceroy of India, Lord Chelmsford, asked Gandhi if he would use his influence to recruit more Indian soldiers. This Gandhi agreed to do. Once again his followers were confused by this decision. Some of his closest friends wrote to Gandhi asking him to reconsider his offer of help. The replies that he gave raise doubts about his views on violence. In a letter to Charlie Andrews, a close friend and a major influence on his non-violent philosophy, he argued: "that under exceptional circumstances, war may have to be resorted to as a necessary evil." He also made the surprising suggestion that after the war, if independence was not granted, Indian soldiers could be employed against the British.

Gandhi's recruiting campaign amongst the Indian peasants was unsuccessful. They could not understand how the man who advocated non-violence in the struggle for independence could now make speeches in favour of them joining the army to fight Germany.

Unlike when he campaigned against unfair taxes and harsh employers, Gandhi received little hospitality from the peasants. Moving from village to village by foot, he was forced to spend most nights sleeping in the open fields. After several months of campaigning, Gandhi had to admit he had only persuaded a hundred men to join the armed forces. This campaign had been a disaster and had severely undermined Gandhi's status as a political and spiritual leader.

Gandhi's belief that the Indians' willingness to help the war effort would be rewarded by political concessions proved to be unfounded. The end of the war revealed that the British government was more afraid than grateful. The Russian Revolution had illustrated what disillusioned peasants, led by determined political leaders, could achieve. Rather than introducing reforms, the British administration were more concerned about suppressing what they described as the 'Bolshevik Menace'.

In March, 1919, a law was passed in India that gave the authorities power to arrest and imprison people who made speeches or published materials that could lead to "public excitement or a breach of the peace."

Gandhi's reaction was to advocate a one day 'General Strike' on April 6. He also openly sold copies of his book 'Hind Swaraj' which with its demands for self-rule, broke the new government regulations. The authorities waited, frightened what would happen if they arrested Gandhi. They were fully aware that Gandhi was a restraining influence on the Indian community and without his leadership, his supporters might resort to violence.

In some areas of India, people were not convinced that passive resistance was the answer to the oppressive laws being introduced by the British authorities . In the large town of Amritsar, a group of Indians who had been upset by the arrest of their leaders, burnt down the town hall and post office.

Brigadier General Reginald Dyer, who had only just arrived to take command of the army in Amritsar, decided to ban all public meetings in the town. Town criers were used to inform the people of Amritsar, but it was later discovered that they were not given instructions to read the order in places where most people would have heard them.

Two days later, a Sikh religious festival went ahead as planned. When General Dyer heard about the festival he took ninety soldiers to Jallianwalla Bagh, the place where the meeting was to be held. Positioning the men on high ground he gave instructions for the soldiers to fire into the crowd until they ran out of ammunition. No warning was given and when the riflemen had exhausted their supply of bullets ten minutes later, 379 Indians lay dead or dying. Another thousand were seriously wounded. Giving instructions to the soldiers not to tend the wounded, General Dyer marched his soldiers out of the square.

General Dyer then imposed martial law on Amritsar. This involved strict censorship and a curfew. Indians who broke these regulations were whipped. In a street where a white woman had been attacked by a group of Indians, local people were forced to crawl on their bellies.

The censorship was effective and Indian leaders did not hear of the massacre until several weeks later. The first Gandhi heard of it was in June. Initially, Gandhi refused to believe the stories he heard about the Massacre in Amritsar. He did not consider it possible for a British General to instruct his soldiers to kill Indians in cold blood.

The Massacre of Amritsar was a turning point in the Indian struggle for independence, It revealed the measures that the British were willing to employ in order to maintain control of India. The British were no longer seen as misguided leaders. The Indians realised that under pressure, the British authorities were willing to resort to acts of extreme violence.

Campaigns 1920-23

The Amritsar Massacre horrified Gandhi. His philosophy of 'satyagraha', or non-violent action, had been developed to avoid deaths. Gandhi was now aware that any strategy that encouraged massive street demonstrations was bound to lead to violence. He therefore decided to develop a new plan of action against the British government. The plan involved four elements: a return of all titles, honours and medals granted by the British; Indians who worked for the government to withdraw their labour; Indian soldiers to refuse to serve in the armed forces and finally, and most importantly, the non-payment of all taxes to the British.

There were two main advantages of this strategy. Firstly, it avoided street confrontations between large numbers of Indians and the British authorities and therefore reduced the possibility of violence. Secondly, if the Indian community obeyed Gandhi's instructions, the British government would find it impossible to impose its rule on India.

The strategy was not a success. The campaign came to a halt when the majority of the lawyers, teachers and civil servants who worked for the government failed to withdraw their labour.

Gandhi and the Congress Party then turned their attention to the importation of cloth. For many years Gandhi had been encouraging Indian peasants to return to the practice of spinning yarn in their homes. Gandhi himself could often be found busy on his spinning-wheel. He even spun when making speeches to large crowds. He told them that: "the spinning-wheel is an emblem of peace and ahimsa". Gandhi was particularly keen for men to take up spinning. He knew that when men were without work they often spent their time drinking alcohol. Gandhi had always objected to this on both moral and economic grounds and hoped that in times of unemployment, working on the spinning-wheel would keep their minds off drink.

Importing British cloth, Gandhi claimed, had not only destroyed the Indian tradition of spinning, but had severely damaged the country's economy. By organising the burning of foreign cloth and encouraging peasants to return to spinning, Gandhi hoped for a return to the situation before the arrival of the British.

Gandhi saw himself as the representative of the Indian peasant. In the years that were to follow he attempted to get as close as possible to the lives of the poor. In 1921, he decided to abandon the practice of wearing a skull cap, long dhots (loincloth) and shirt. Instead he adopted the clothes of a poor peasant. From now on he would travel the country, naked except for a small loincloth and a shawl if the weather was cold.

In November, 1921, the Prince of Wales visited India. When he arrived in Bombay, Gandhi instructed all Indians to inform the British Prince of their desire for independence by going on strike. Although they were ordered not to resort to violence, the strike soon got out of hand. Shops selling foreign cloth were looted and set on fire. Policemen who attempted to stop the rioting were attacked and two died later in hospital.

Worse was to follow. In February, 1922, a large procession of Gandhi's supporters were fired on by police at Chauri Chaura. The constables were then chased back to the local police station. When the police ran out of ammunition, the crowd set fire to the building. As they came running out, the angry crowd caught and killed twenty-two of the policemen.

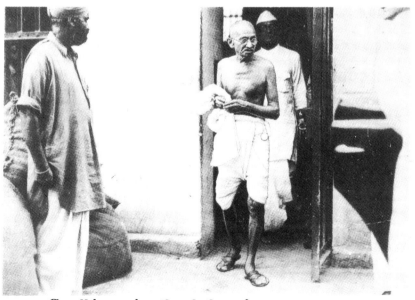

Gandhi wearing the clothes of a poor peasant

40

Gandhi was horrified by these events, especially when he heard how the crowd who killed the policeman had been chanting "victory to Mahatma Gandhi". To avoid further bloodshed, Gandhi called off his civil-disobedience campaign. The other leaders of the Congress Party were furious. They believed that the British, in an attempt to end the violence, were close to making concessions on self-rule.

With the Congress leaders in disarray and the masses disillusioned, the British authorities felt strong enough to arrest Gandhi for sedition. Gandhi took full responsibility for the deaths that had taken place. He told the court: "I wish to endorse all the blame which the learned Advocate-General had thrown on my shoulders... it is impossible for me to disassociate myself from the diabolical crimes of Chauri Chaura or the mad outrages of Bombay. He is quite right when he says that as a man of responsibility, a man having received a fair share of experience of this world, I should have known the consequences of every one of my acts. I knew that I was playing with fire." As a measure of his guilt, Gandhi asked for the maximum penalty possible. The judge responded by sentencing him to six years imprisonment.

Hindus and Muslims

The imprisonment of Gandhi brought a temporary halt in the fight for Indian independence. Gandhi spent his time in Yeravda Jail deep in thought about his future political activities. His opponents had often accused him of being a dictator, but the events in Bombay and Chauri Chaura revealed that he did not have full control over his followers. Unless he could obtain their strict obedience, there was always the danger that any demonstrations that he organised would develop into violence.

In January, 1924, acute appendicitis nearly killed Gandhi. While recovering in hospital, the British government decided to release him from prison. However, Gandhi did not return to active politics until his original sentence finished in 1928. Between 1924 and 1928, Gandhi spent his time travelling to some of India's 500,000 villages. At this time his main concern was to reduce the tension amongst the different groups in India. As well as 220 million Hindus and 70 million Muslims, there were a variety of other religious groups such as Christians, Sikhs, Jews and Buddhists. Gandhi, like other Indian nationalists, believed that the British government had encouraged divisions amongst the different communities. 'Divide and Rule' had been a strategy that the British had often employed to control its Empire.

Gandhi was of the opinion that without a united Indian independence movement, self-rule was unlikely to be achieved. As a

Hindu, Gandhi tried hard to gain the support of other religious groups in the country. One way he had attempted was to take up their causes. For example, after the First World War, Gandhi had supported the Muslim campaign to obtain the release from prison of the Sultan of Turkey. The Sultan was regarded as the supreme head of the Muslim community and a considerable amount of anger had been caused by the decision of the British to imprison him after their victory over Turkey in 1918.

To many, Gandhi's support of a man who had forced large numbers of different races to live under his rule, appeared to contradict his political and moral beliefs. However, Gandhi, in an effort to achieve his political objectives, was on occasion, willing to make pragmatic decisions. Gandhi believed that if the Congress Party could recruit large numbers of Muslims into its ranks, the British could not possibly prevent independence taking place.

On several occasions Gandhi protested against acts of violence between Hindus and Muslims by going on fasts. In September, 1924, Muslims massacred 155 Hindus at Kohat. A week later Gandhi started a fast and said it would continue until Hindu and Muslim leaders in the area assured him that these events would not recur. It was not until religious leaders agreed to meet at a unity conference in Delhi and pass a resolution condemning religious violence that Gandhi started eating again. The fast had lasted twenty-one days, the longest that Gandhi had undertaken.

Whenever Gandhi went to a village his message was always the same. As Horace Alexander, who witnessed Gandhi's speeches at this time, has pointed out: "He was concerned to persuade the people of rural India that their basic human interests were all one, and that the deep cleavages which had developed through the centuries between Hindus and Muslims, between caste Hindu and outcaste, so that many villages have, to all intents and purposes, lived in three distinct sections, were basically mischievous and involved a denial of the truth of universal brotherhood."

The Salt Campaign

In December, 1929, Lord Irwin, the Viceroy of India, met the leaders of the Congress Party to discuss the possibility of political reforms. An agreed programme was not reached and it was decided that Gandhi would once again lead a civil disobedience campaign.

Of the eleven suggestions put forward, Gandhi decided to concentrate on the issue of the salt tax. India was well supplied with natural salt but the British government passed laws forcing the Indians to buy the commodity from them. Gandhi argued that all Indians used salt and therefore a campaign against the salt tax would

Gandhi marching to Dandhi

involve everybody. The salt tax was also a clear example of how the British put profit before the interests of the Indian people.

On March 11, 1930, Gandhi and seventy-eight of his followers left the ashram to walk 241 miles to Dandi on the Indian coast. At each village that they came to, Gandhi would stop and make speeches to the local people explaining their campaign. People joined Gandhi's march and soon the procession spread back for two miles.

Tension mounted as Gandhi and his followers moved closer to the coast. Everyone was asking themselves what the British authorities would do when Gandhi broke the government's salt monopoly.

Gandhi, who was now sixty-one years old, marched on average nine miles a day. He was in no hurry as he knew that the longer he took, the more publicity he would receive.

The procession reached Dandi on April 6, the anniversary of the 'Amritsar Massacre'. After a night of prayer and fasting, Gandhi took a small lump of natural salt from the Dandi beach. The police decided to ignore Gandhi's actions and he was not arrested. Although the press were forbidden to print news of Gandhi's campaign, news quickly spread and all over the country, Indians followed Gandhi's example and broke government regulations by taking natural salt from the seashore.

In the next few weeks the British authorities arrested many people for making their own salt. However, they were reluctant to imprison Gandhi because they feared it could lead to large riots and demonstrations.

43

On May 4, Gandhi informed the British authorities that his 2,500 campaigners planned to take possession of the government owned Dharasana saltworks on behalf of the Indian people. That night, Gandhi was arrested. This did not stop the march on the Dharasana saltworks and the next day, a group of volunteers attempted to carry out Gandhi's threat. The saltworks were defended by 400 policemen carrying steel-tipped batons. As the marchers entered land belonging to saltworks, the policemen clubbed them with their batons. As one group was beaten unconscious, the next group moved forward. As they marched they shouted 'Long live the revolution'. Webb Miller, a journalist who was at the salt works, later revealed that not one of the marchers raised their hands to protect themselves. The police were not satisfied with just knocking the marchers to the ground. Probably in an attempt to persuade the salt campaigners watching in the distance not to move forward, the police carried out outrageous acts on the satyagraphis while they were on the floor.

For two hours, Gandhi's salt campaigners marched towards the Dharasana saltworks. Column after column of them were beaten to the ground. An investigation carried out later revealed that two satyagraphis were killed and 290 suffered serious injuries.As one eyewitness remarked afterwards: "All hope of reconciling India with the British Empire is lost forever."

Friends and Companions

There was never a shortage of people arriving at Gandhi's ashram to dedicate their lives to satyagrapha. Some of these people had travelled from other countries after reading about Gandhi in magazine and newspaper articles. Charlie Andrews, a christian missionary, first met Gandhi when he was campaigning in South Africa. Andrews had close contacts with the British authorities and was in a good position to advise Gandhi on the best way to deal with them. Some satyagraphis were jealous of Andrews and attempts were made to persuade Gandhi that he was a British spy. Although Andrews remained a loyal supporter of Gandhi he was not afraid to disagree with him. As a pacifist he was especially critical of Gandhi's involvement in recruitment for the armed forces.

Mahadev Desai, a lawyer, met Gandhi in 1917. Gandhi was immediately drawn to the man. He was later to say to him: "It takes me only a little while to judge people. I have been looking for the one person to whom I will one day be able to entrust my work." Gandhi described Desai as his 'perfect son'.

Desai became Gandhi's secretary. One of the reasons that Desai was selected for this task was his beautiful handwriting. Gandhi had

Nehru sharing a joke with Gandhi

always been ashamed of his 'scrawl' and after Desai became his secretary, Gandhi dictated all his letters to him to write. This was some task as Gandhi was known to write as many as fifty letters a day. One historian has claimed that if all the letters Gandhi wrote were ever published, it would involve the printing of at least 100 large books.

Jawaharlal Nehru was Gandhi's closest political ally. Nehru, who came from a rich and privileged background, became an active member of the Indian Congress Party after the Amritsar Massacre. Nehru visited the Soviet Union and was impressed by the achievements of communism. Nehru eventually became the leader of the socialist wing of the Congress Party and influenced Gandhi's views on the redistribution of wealth.

The most important figure in his later life was Manubehn, the granddaughter of Gandhi's uncle. Manubehn had been arrested at the age of fourteen for taking part in the activities of the independence movement. A year later she became Gandhi's nurse. They became extremely close and Gandhi told his friends that Manubehn had become the daughter whom he had never had.

Some of Gandhi's close advisers became concerned when they discovered that young Manubehn was sharing the same bed as Gandhi. Rumours began to circulate and Gandhi was forced to write a series of letters to his supporters explaining how he was still maintaining his vow of chastity. It was later revealed that Gandhi, who suffered from shivering fits, often arranged for women to share his bed to keep him warm.

Round Table Talks

In 1919, the House of Commons had passed the 'India Act'. Although the British government retained control of central government in India, the 1919 Act did allow Indians to have influence over some aspects of local government. This Act was unpopular with the Congress Party who demanded the same rights as the 'white' commonwealth. Countries with large white populations such as Australia, New Zealand, Canada and South Africa had all achieved Dominion status within the Empire. Arthur Balfour, the British Prime Minister in 1926, defined 'Dominion' as : "autonomous communities within the British Empire, equal in status, in no way subordinate... united by a common allegiance to the Crown." The Indian Congress Party accused the British government of racism in its willingness to grant dominion status t countries with large white populations but refusal to give the same rights to the 'black' commonwealth.

Gandhi's campaign had shown the strength of feeling about self-rule and the British government agreed to take another look at the possibility of granting India dominion status. In 1931, Congress leaders, including Gandhi, were released from prison and invited to London for talks on the subject.

Rather than stay at the hotel provided, Gandhi opted to live in a small room in the poor, working-class district of Bow. He said he wanted to get to know the 'real' people of Britain. Gandhi had not got on very well with the members of the aristocracy that he had met. This was partly due to Gandhi's criticisms of the British Empire. When Gandhi met King George V he was rebuked like a naughty boy. The King had been annoyed with him ever since he had organised the boycott of his son's visit to India in 1921. King George V gave his Indian visitor a stern lecture and concluded with the words: "I won't have you stirring up trouble in my Empire."

The British government refused to negotiate with the Indian leaders as equals and the 'Round-Table' talks as they became known, ended in failure. However, as far as Gandhi was concerned, the journey was not wasted. He decided to visit the textile workers of Lancashire. The Congress Party's decision to boycott foreign

Gandhi meets Lancashire cotton workers.

cloth had increased unemployment amongst textile workers in Britain. Gandhi felt they needed an explanation . When he arrived in Lancashire, the main area producing cotton in Britain, there was a large crowd to greet him. Gandhi told them how British cloth imports were creating large-scale poverty in India. He went on to compare the life-styles of the unemployed worker in Britain and the Indian peasant. As one man in the crowd said afterwards: "I am one of the unemployed but if I was in India I would say the same thing that Gandhi is saying." The reception that he received after his speech suggested that Gandhi was more popular with the working-classes than the aristocracy. Wherever he went, crowds cheered him. They were not used to political leaders mixing freely with the masses and they appreciated his warmth and openness. The British working-class could see that Gandhi was indeed a man of the people.

Soon after Gandhi and the other Congress leaders arrived back in India they were arrested and placed once again in prison. For the next few years Gandhi spent long periods in prison. During this time he engaged in several fasts. The reasons for these fasts either involved the demand for self-rule or better treatment for the untouchables. The British authorities, frightened that Gandhi might die in prison and become a martyr, usually released him soon after he started a fast. When he started eating again he was promptly re-arrested. These 'Cat and Mouse' tactics had previously been employed by the British government against the suffragettes.

In 1935, the House of Commons passed another 'India Act'. This proposed dividing India into eleven provincial states. Gandhi was opposed to this Act as he believed it would create disunity amongst Indians. He saw the possibility of a strong Congress Party made up of both Hindus and Muslims disappearing.

Muhammed Ali Jinnah, the leading Muslim in the Congress Party, left in 1934. Gandhi wanted time to try to persuade him to rejoin before the elections took place in 1937. He failed and people voted in the elections on religious lines. The decision by the governments in most states not to appoint Muslim ministers, further exasperated the problem. Jinnah and his supporters began to talk about the need for a separate Muslim state within India.

The Second World War

The Congress Party was highly critical of British foreign policy in the 1930s. They accused the British government of being sympathetic to fascism after its policy of appeasement towards Hitler. When Neville Chamberlain signed the Munich Agreement with Hitler in 1938, Gandhi wrote: "Europe has sold her soul for the sake of a 'seven days' earthly existence. The peace that Europe gained at Munich is a triumph of violence."

When Germany invaded Czechoslavakia, Gandhi wrote to President Benes advising the use of satyagraha against the Nazis. Gandhi also suggested the same strategy to the Jews in Germany. Gandhi was of the opinion that passive resistance would rouse world opinion against Hitler and the Nazis.

The Indian Congress Party was completely opposed to fascism but they were furious when the Viceroy of India declared war on Germany without consulting them first. With this decision, the Viceroy made it clear that India was subservient to the British government.

The Congress Party offered to support the British government if they were willing to issue a statement that this was a war in favour of democracy throughout the world and not just Europe. When Britain declined this offer, all members of the Congress Party resigned from office. Many of these posts were filled by the Muslim League, thus creating even more conflict between the two religious groups.

Some members of the Congress League demanded a massive civil disobedience campaign. The leaders of the Congress Party were in a difficult position. They wanted to make use of Britain's weakness, but did not want to do anything that would help a German victory. A compromise was drawn up where people would be selected to commit individual acts of civil disobedience. These people were arrested and placed in prison without trial. By May, 1941, over 2,500 people had been arrested.

In 1942, Japan was able to take control of Malaya, Singapore and Hong Kong. It appeared possible that Japan would soon be launching an invasion of India. Sir Stafford Cripps, a socialist and supporter of Indian Independence, was sent by Winston Churchill to meet the Congress leaders. In exchange for their support, the British government offered reform of the role of the Viceroy and a commitment that India would be granted dominion status once the war with Germany was over. The Congress Party had learnt its lesson from the First World War and was unwilling to comply with the government demands in return for the promise of a reward in the distant future. Although the Congress leaders liked Sir Stafford Cripps, they did not trust Winston Churchill, the Prime Minister, who had been one of the strongest opponents of Indian Independence during the 1920s and 30s. He was particularly hostile to Gandhi whom he described as a:"nauseating, seditious Middle Temple lawyer... posing as a fakir (holy man)".

In August 1942, the Congress Party endorsed a new 'Quit India' campaign. Gandhi was chosen to organise the campaign. Within hours of the announcement, Gandhi and his fellow leaders were arrested and put in prison. Here they stayed without trial until the end of the war.

Five days after being placed in prison, Mahadev Desai, Gandhi's secretary, died. Kasturbhai, who had been arrested at the same time as Gandhi, also became very ill. She was now seventy-two and had a weak heart. The shock of being imprisoned seriously affected her health. The prison doctors warned Gandhi that his wife was seriously ill and that the only thing that could save her was penicillin injections. Gandhi, who had always opposed modern medicine, refused permission for the injections to be given. His son, Devadas, pleaded with him to let the doctors try this new 'wonder drug' but Gandhi refused to change his mind.

Knowing that Kasturbhai was going to die, an attempt was made to find her son Harilal, who had left the family home thirty three years previously, after an argument with Gandhi. Harilal was found and brought to his dying mother. Harilal had become an alcoholic and the sight of her drunk son deeply upset Kasturbhai. Gandhi was so angry that he wrote an article in his newspaper, the 'Harijan', denouncing his son.

Gandhi was with his wife when she died. Kasturbhai told him: "I am going now. No one should cry after I have gone. I am at peace." Gandhi held her in his arms and they sang their favourite hymn 'Ramadhm' together and by the time the hymn was finished, Kasturbhai was dead.

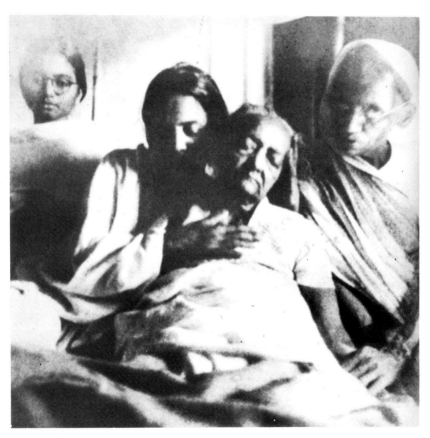

Photograph taken of Kasturbhai in prison just before her death. From left to right, Manubehn, Sushila Nayyar, Kasturbhai and Gandhi.

Gandhi in 1946   **Jawaharlal Nehru**

Partition

As soon as the war was over the Congress leaders were released. The possibility of Indian independence increased with the Labour Party's overwhelming election victory in 1945. Winston Churchill was replaced by Clement Attlee as Prime Minister. The Labour Party had been in favour of Indian independence for some time so as soon as they gained power they arranged for negotiations to start.

The main problem was not the the granting of self-rule but dealing with the conflict between the Congress Party and the Muslin League. Muhammed Ali Jinnah, the leader of the Muslim League, now demanded that the six provinces that had a Muslim majority - Baluchistan, Sind, the Punjab, Bengal, Assam and the North-West Frontier - should join together to form an independent Muslim state called Pakistan. Gandhi was horrified. This proposal was diametrically opposed to his belief in a united India. Gandhi wanted the Indian government to be headed by Jawaharlal Nehru, an atheist who was respected by both Hindu and Muslim communities. If that was unacceptable, Gandhi said he preferred Jinnah, a Muslim, to form the new government than the development of two separate nations.

Those involved in the negotiations failed to reach a solution that pleased all parties. The Viceroy had no choice but to ask Nehru, the

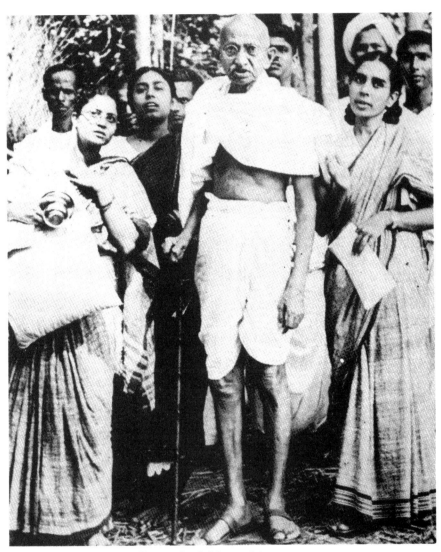

Gandhi visiting villages

leader of the largest political party, to form a government. Jinnah's reaction to this was to encourage Muslims to show their opposition to the new government by taking 'Direct Action'. Hindus in Muslim provinces were massacred. Hindus responded by murdering Muslims. In the Calcutta region alone, over 4,000 people were killed.

Gandhi's response to these massacres was to take his followers to as many villages as possible. He placed a satyagrahi in each village and instructed them to keep the peace. In some cases this worked but still the killings went on. 'Direct Action' had the desired effect. The British government became convinced that a united India was unattainable. Lord Mountbatten was appointed as the last Viceroy of India. When he arrived in India he brought with him the news that the different parties only had until June, 1948 to reach an agreement. Jinnah refused to change his demand for an independent Muslim state. Gandhi thought back to the 1920s when Hindus and Muslims were united in their demands for an independent India. Now it was too late and reluctantly, Gandhi and the other Congress leaders agreed that partition was the only way to stop the killing.

Independence

It was decided that on August 15, 1947, India and Pakistan would become two self-governing, independent states. The news resulted in the mass migration of Hindus to India and Muslims to Pakistan. The hostility between the two groups was now so deep that Hindu and Muslim travellers were taken from the trains by armed mobs and killed. An estimated one million people were murdered in this way during the weeks leading up to independence.

Leaders of both religions appealed for these massacres to end but people appeared to be determined to obtain revenge for previous killings. Gandhi was especially concerned that Independence Day would be celebrated by further massacres. Calcutta, which had seen large-scale killings, was considered to be a particular problem. Gandhi therefore decided to spend the period before the Declaration of Independence touring Calcutta appealing for calm.

When he arrived in Calcutta, Gandhi sought out Suhrawardy, the leader of the Muslim community. Gandhi proposed that the two men lived together in one of the abandoned homes in the Muslim area of the city. Suhrawardy agreed, but when news reached the militant young Hindus in Calcutta they became very angry and the house was quickly surrounded. The militant Hindus were also hostile to Gandhi as they felt he had betrayed them by agreeing to the setting up of Pakistan.

Gandhi left the house to speak to the large crowd that had assembled: "If I am to be killed, it is you who can kill me. After all, I am an old man now. I have very few days to live. You want to force me to leave this place. I never submit to force of any kind whatsoever! It is not my nature." The crowd was impressed by how this frail old man of 78 had the courage to stand up and defy these young armed men. They not only agreed to go away but left some young Hindus behind to protect the two men.

The next day an even larger crowd arrived. They demanded to

Lord and Lady Mountbatten with Gandhi in 1947

see Suhrawardy. Gandhi and Suhrawardy went out to meet the crowd together. Someone in the crowd asked if Suhrawardy was responsible for the massacres the previous August. He admitted his guilt and proposed that a new effort should be made for the two groups to live peacefully together. Eventually, when the crowd had calmed down, Gandhi and Suhrawardy arranged a united march of 10,000 Hindus and Muslims through the streets of Calcutta.

On Independence Day, Gandhi and Suhrawardy drove through Calcutta together. The crowds waved the new Indian national flag and chanted "Hindus and Muslims are brothers" and "Long live Gandhi". For that day anyway, the two groups lived in peace.

Gandhi received telegrams from all over the world congratulating him on winning his long battle. Several referred to him as the 'Father of the Nation'. However, his friends observed that he was not happy in this moment of triumph. All his political life he had employed non-violent methods to obtain his objectives. India had her independence but it had been at a terrible price. As well as congratulatory telegrams, Gandhi had been receiving reports of large-scale massacres all over India. In the words of the Indian historian, Humagun Kabir: "Freedom had been bought at the cost of unity and peace."

Gandhi's Death

After independence Gandhi moved to a new home in Delhi. He lived quietly with Manubehn and a few close friends. The killings continued and on January 13, 1948, he announced that he would fast until death unless the leaders of the Hindu and Muslim extremist groups signed an agreement promising to end the violence. Gandhi was no longer fit enough to go on a long fast. After only a few days he became delirious and his doctors told his family that he was close to death. On January, 18, the leaders of the extremist groups agreed to sign. The fast had taken its toll and it was several days before he could move around the house again.

Once a day, Gandhi would leave his house and meet the people in his prayer garden. There around 300 people would pray together and afterwards listen to Gandhi give a sermon. On January, 20, Gandhi spoke against the lynchings of black men in America. While he was speaking a bomb exploded. Gandhi was unhurt. The man who threw the bomb was quickly arrested. At the local police station he admitted that he was a militant Hindu who wanted to kill Gandhi for encouraging peace and friendship with the Muslims.

Several days after the assassination attempt, Gandhi spoke to Manubehn about how he believed that God had decided that he should have a violent death. He told her he would be shot and that

Gandhi just before his death   Nathuram Godse

he would die lying on her lap with a smile on his face. Only if he died this way, he informed Manubehn: "should you say I was a true Mahatma".

The next day, while he was walking in his prayer garden, a man came out of the crowds and bent down in front of Gandhi as if in prayer. He then got up and shot Gandhi three times, once in the abdomen and twice in the chest. Manubehn placed his head on her lap and watched the life flow out of his body. She said later that he died with a smile on his face.

The killer's name was Nathuram Godse. At his trial he explained in detail why he had killed Gandhi: "My respect for the Mahatma was deep and depthless. It therefore gave me no pleasure to kill him... I bowed to him first, then at point blank range fired three successive shots and killed him. My provocation was his constant and consistent pandering to the Muslims... I have no private grudge against him. I only considered the future of the nature."

Nathuram Godse was found guilty and sentenced to death. Gandhi's son Ramdas informed the court that his father would have wanted Godse's life spared. The judge in charge of the case rejected this plea and Godse and his accomplice, Narayan Apte, were executed on November 15, 1949.

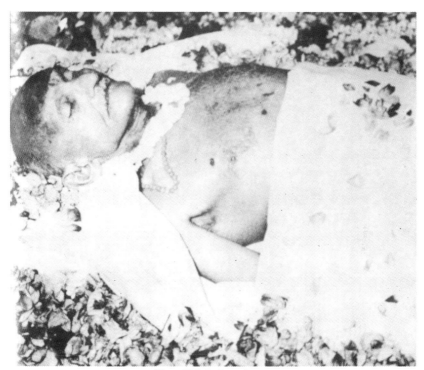

Gandhi lying in state

The Individual in History

Gandhi

Source Material

Unit 1: The British Raj

The British had taught them not to think for themselves, and not to be self-dependent for their clothes and their tools. "We command, you obey," said the British, "for we know what is good for you; we will supply you with better clothes and tools than you can make, and you can buy them at world-market prices." "But you need not obey," said Gandhi, "you can be wholly independent. Moreover, if you make your own clothes and your own tools, you will be beginning the fight against your abject poverty. You can do it for yourselves."

(A) Horace Alexander, 'Consider India', (1961)

I was a great believer in the maximum display of force at the very beginning to try and overawe people. I was also a great believer in using force effectively if it had to be used at all. I didn't believe in firing one or two rounds. I used to say to my magistrate, 'If you ever have to open fire, fire at least five rounds, nobody is going to be able to prove that was excessive'. Another thing that we were taught, which is now forgotten, was never to fire over the head of a crowd. If you open fire, make sure that it is effective so that people are seen to fall and the mob takes fright.

(B) P. Moon, Indian Civil Servant, radio interview, (1975)

(C) The wedding of the Maharajah of Patiala, (1932)

I can honestly say that at the time when we were living and working in India, there was absolutely no feeling of exploitation, no feeling of being wicked imperialists. In fact in those days we did not think imperialists were necessarily wicked. We thought we were bringing enlightenment to backward parts of the world.
(D) **Lady Birdwood, British resident, radio interview, (1975)**

We were proud of being British. My father, when he heard 'God Save the King' being sung, even away in the distance, stood up and we had to stand up with him. That is what we thought of the British Raj and it came as a shock to us when it ended.
(E) **Irene Edwards, British resident, radio interview, (1975)**

I remember once returning from leave in England in the twenties. I went on to the train in Bombay and discovered that the other berth was occupied by an Indian. I am sorry to say that by that time I had become affected by the mentality of the ruling class in India and I said to the station-master, 'I want to have the gentlemen ejected.' He spoke absolutely perfect English and he could have taught me a great deal about India. It is one of the incidents of my life of which I am most ashamed. But you have to remember that in those days army officers did not associate with Indians of any class other than the servant class, to whom they just gave orders.
(F) **John Morris, Indian Army Officer, radio interview, (1975)**

My first glimpse of an Englishman was in the person of the Deputy Commissioner of the district. Astride a horse, he halted before the school for a bare five minutes... I was charmed by his personality, so handsome and well-groomed, the very embodiment of the Raj. Soon, in a sudden fit of hostile reaction, I was asking myself:"Why is he here?" All that had been hammered into my mind about the blessings of the British Raj had mysteriously evaporated. Was this due to the childhood prejudice against the beef-eating foreigner or the faint stirring of that spirit which was to find expression in the years to come in the Gandhian revolution?
(G) **Durga Das, 'India', (1969)**

see page 12

1. *How does source G help to support the point of view expressed in source A?*

2. *Sources B, C, D, E and F tell us about the attitudes of the British people who lived in India?*

3. *Four of these sources are radio interviews. Discuss the advantages and disadvantages of interviews as historical source material.*

61

Unit 2: The Empire

What is power worth if it is founded on vice, on ignorance, and on misery; if we hold it only by violating the most sacred duties which as governors we owe to the governed... We are free, we are civilised, to little purpose, if we grudge to any portion of the human race an equal measure of freedom and civilisation. Are we to keep the people ignorant that we may keep them submissive? Or do we think that we can give them knowledge without wakening ambition?

(A) Lord Macaulay, speech, House of Commons, (1833)

When the existence of the Empire was threatened in 1899 by the Boer challenge, I offered my services to it, raised a volunteer ambulance corps and served in several actions that took place for the relief of Ladysmith. Similarly in 1906, at the time of the Zulu 'revolt', I raised a stretcher-bearer party and served till the end of the 'rebellion'... When the war broke out in 1914 between England and Germany, I raised a volunteer ambulance corps in London, consisting of the then resident Indians in London... Lastly, in India when a special appeal was made at the War Conference in Delhi in 1918 by Lord Chelmsford for recruits, I struggled at the cost of my health to raise a corps in Kheda... I was actuated by the belief that it was possible by such services to gain a status of full equality in the Empire for my countrymen.The first shock came in the shape of the Rowlatt Act - a law designed to rob the people of all real freedom... then followed the Punjab horrors beginning with the massacre at Amritsar and culminating in crawling orders, public flogging and other indescribable humiliations.

(B) Gandhi, speech in court, (March, 1922)

No empire intoxicated with the red wine of power and plunder of weaker races has yet lived long in the world, and this British Empire, which is based upon organised exploitation of physically weaker races of the earth and upon a continuous exhibition of brute force, cannot live if there is a just God ruling the universe... It is high time that the British people were made to realise that the fight that was commenced in 1920 is a fight to the finish.

(C) Gandhi, 'Young India', newspaper, (February, 1922)

We have as good a right to be in India as anyone there... Our Government is not an irresponsible Government... It is incomparably the best Government that India has ever had or ever will have... We hope once and for all to kill the idea that the British in India are aliens moving, with many apologies, out of the country as soon as they have been able to set up any government organism to take their place.

(D) Winston Churchill, speech, House of Commons, (1935)

(E) "But how about keeping the brute?", Punch, (1858)

Though I hold the British rule in India to be a curse, I do not, therefore, consider Englishmen in general to be worse than any other people on earth. I have the privilege of claiming many Englishmen as dearest friends. Indeed much that I have learnt of the evil of British rule is due to the writings of frank and courageous Englishmen who have not hesitated to tell the unpalatable truth about that rule.

(F) Gandhi, letter to Lord Irwin, Viceroy of India, (1930)

One-fifth of the human race has been brought under the British heel by means that will not bear scrutiny... Ours is an unarmed revolt against British rule. But whether we convert them or not, we are determined to make their rule impossible by non-violent non-cooperation. It is a method in its nature undefeatable.

(G) Gandhi, letter to Hitler, (December, 1941)

1. *What evidence is there in this unit that Gandhi changed his mind about the British Empire?*

2. *Describe and explain the different views on the British rule of India expressed in sources A and D*

3. *Explain the meaning of source E.*

4. *Why did Gandhi consider it necessary to write to Hitler in 1941?*

Unit 3: Satyagraha

Passive resistance... is superior to the force of arms... ... Even a man weak in body is capable of offering this resistance. One man can offer it just as well as millions. Both men and women can indulge in it... Control over the mind is alone necessary, and when that is attained, man is free like the king of the forest and his very glance withers the enemy.
(A) Gandhi, 'Hind Swarf', (1909)

I know that in embarking on non-violence, I shall be running what might be fairly termed a mad risk, but the victories of truth have never been won without risks, often of the gravest character. Conversion of a nation that has consciously preyed upon another far more numerous, far more ancient and no less cultured than itself, is worth any amount of risk... my ambition is no less than to convert the British people through non-violence and thus make them see the wrong they have done to India.
(B) Gandhi, letter to Lord Irwin, Viceroy of India, (1930)

1. A Satyagrahi, i.e. a civil resister, will harbour no anger.
2. He will suffer the anger of an opponent.
3. In doing so he will put up with assaults from the opponent, never retaliate, but he will not submit, out of fear of punishment or the like, to any order given in anger.
4. When any person in authority seeks to arrest a civil resister, he will voluntarily submit to the arrest and he will not resist the attachment or removal of his own property, if any, when it is sought to be confiscated by the authorities.
(C) Gandhi, Commandments for a Satyagrahi, (1940)

Gandhi himself admitted in 1930, after more than ten years, that few, if any, of his followers have understood the principles of 'satyagraha' or have developed necessary strengths to exercise it. Anyone conversant with human nature would hardly expect anything else. But what is worse still, few even among his chief disciples or followers, really believed in the idea of 'satyagraha'... Gandhi himself knew this quite well, for he said, "If India possessed the sword, I know that India would not have listened to this gospel" of non-violence. It is thus quite clear that whatever we might think of the virtue of 'satyagraha" as a principle, it was never put to the test. It may be doubted whether there were even four hundred real 'satyagrahis' out of the 400 millions of Indians. There was thus no real 'satyagraha' campaign in India, and of course, no effect of it upon Britain.
(D) R.C. Majumdar, 'India's Struggle for Freedom', (1961)

(E) 'Frankenstein of the East', (1930)

'Satyagraha' was a definite, though non-violent, form of resistance to what was considered wrong. ... It put us on our best behaviour and seemed to put the adversary in the wrong.
(F) Jawaharlal Nehru, 'Toward Freedom', (1936)

His simple life, his vegetarian diet, his goat's milk, his day of silence every week, his habit of squatting on the floor instead of sitting on the chair, his loincloth - in fact everything connected with him - has marked him out as one of the eccentric Mahatmas of old and has brought him nearer to the people... Born in another country he might have been a complete misfit. What, for instance, would he have done in a country like Russia or Germany or Italy? His doctrine of non-violence would have led him to the cross or to the mental hospital.
(G) Subhas Chandra Bose, 'The Indian Struggle', (1935),

see pages 27-31 and 37

1. *Select passages from sources A, B and C that help to explain Nehru's last sentence in source F.*

2. *Explain the meaning of source E.*

3. *Choose the three sources in this unit that are critical of Satyagraha. Explain in your own words what these three sources are saying.*

Unit 4: First World War

When two nations are fighting, the duty of a devotee of ahimsa is to stop the war. He who is not equal to that duty, he who has no power of resisting war, he who is not qualified to resist war, may take part in war... I had hoped to improve my status and that of my people through the British Empire. Whilst in England I was enjoying the protection of the British Fleet, and taking shelter as I did under its armed might, I was directly participating in its potential violence... I could participate in the war on the side of the Empire and thereby acquire the capacity and fitness for resisting the war. I lacked this capacity and fitness, so I thought there was nothing for it but to serve in the war.
(A) Gandhi, 'An Autobiography', (1927)

When Gandhi arrived in London on August 6, 1914... newsboys were shouting about the invasion of Belgium and the streets were crowded with people waving Union Jacks... Almost at once Gandhi decided to offer his services to the War Office. A circular letter was sent to the Indians he knew in London, suggesting that they should place themselves unconditionally at the disposal of the authorities... he wrote to the Under Secretary of State for India, saying that his fellow Indians desired "to share the responsibilities of membership of their great Empire... To the argument that this was a heaven-sent opportunity for the Indians to press their claim for independence he answered that the Indians must first show their goodwill by standing beside England in their hour of need.
(B) Robert Payne, 'Mahatma Gandhi', (1969)

Like most English-educated Indians of his generation, Gandhi was then (during the First World War) a loyal and moderate nationalist... He was "a lover" of the British Empire, because he thought it was on the whole doing good to his country. He believed that Indians could rise to their full stature within and with the help of the Empire. He wanted his country to qualify for equal partnership in the Empire by loyal service and sacrifice... Throughout World War 1 Gandhi laboured strenuously in the cause of the defence of the Empire. He preached "absolutely unconditional and wholehearted cooperation with the government on the part of educated India" in the war effort and emphasised what he considered to be the elementary truth that if the Empire perished, with it would perish their cherished political aspirations for their own country.
(C) S.R. Mehrotra,'India Quarterly' magazine, (1961)

From the military point of view one of India's most important assets is an almost inexhaustible supply of manpower... Without this help it would have been difficult to have won the last two wars.
(D) British Chiefs of Staff, (1946)

Hindu and Muslim will be fighting side by side with British soldiers and our gallant French allies... You will be the first Indian soldiers of the King Emperor who will have the honour of showing in Europe that the sons of India have lost none of their ancient martial instincts... In battle you will remember that your religions enjoin on you that to give your life doing your duty is your highest reward... You will fight for your King Emperor and your faith, so that history will record the doings of India's sons and your children will proudly tell of the deeds of their fathers.

(E) King George V, message to Indian soldiers, (1914)

The heavy fighting in France and Flanders at the beginning of World War 1 gave the men from India many opportunities to display their courage. Fighting in a completely strange environment, far from home, cold, wet, and subjected to a far more heavily armed enemy than they could have ever imagined, the men of the Indian Corps in the British Expeditionary Force displayed courage of the highest order.

(F) T.A. Heathcote, 'The Indian Army', (1974)

Today for the first time we had to fight against the Indians and the devil knows those brown rascals are not to be underrated. At first we spoke with contempt of the Indians. Today we learned to look on them in a different light - the devil knows what the English had put into those fellows... With a fearful shouting thousands of these brown forms rushed upon us... At a hundred metres we opened a destructive fire which mowed down hundreds but in spite of that the others advanced... in no time they were in our trenches and truly those brown enemies were not to be despised.

(G) German soldier, letter, (1915)

India waited after the war; resentful, rather aggressive, not very helpful, but still `expectant. Within a few months, the first fruits of the new British policy, so eagerly waited for, appeared in the shape of a proposal to pass special laws to control the revolutionary movement. Instead of more freedom, there was to be more repression. These bills were based on the report of a committee and were known as the Rowlatt Bills... They gave great powers to the government and the police to arrest, keep in prison without trial any person they disapproved of or suspected.

(H) Jawaharal Nehru, 'Toward Freedom', (1941)

see pages 33-34

1. *"Gandhi was a pacifist". Does the evidence in this unit support this statement?*

2. *What arguments does King George V use to encourage Indians to fight in the First World War?*

3. *Why were Indians "expectant" (source H) after the war? Use sources from this unit to support your answer.*

Unit 5: Indigo Dispute

Champaran lies between Nepal and the Himalayas... Its area is about 3,500 square miles, its population a couple of million, mainly Hindu and almost entirely rural...In 1917 Champaran was a preserve of English planters who, for more than half a century, had owned most of the arable land and imposed an almost feudal regime... Under a contract system known as 'tinkathia', the tenants had to plant three-twentieths of their holdings with indigo, and hand over the indigo harvest as part of their rent. It went into dye factories owned by the English.
(A) Geoffrey Ashe, 'Gandhi', (1968)

It should be remembered that no one knew me in Champaran, being far up north of the Ganges, and right at the foot of the Himalayas in close proximity to Nepal, was cut off from the rest of India... No political work had yet been done amongst them. The world outside Champaran was not known to them. And yet they received me as though we had been age-long friends... The Secretary of the Planters' Association told me plainly that I was an outsider and that I had no business to come between the planters and their tenants... I politely told him that I did not regard myself as an outsider, and that I had every right to inquire into the conditions of the tenants if they desired me to do so.
(B) Gandhi, 'My Autobiography', (1927)

(C) Buffalo-cart (1927)

68

We may look on Mr. Gandhi as an idealist, a fanatic, or a revolutionary according to our particular opinions. But to the peasants he is their liberator, and they credit him with extraordinary powers. He moves about in the villages asking them to lay their grievances before him, and he is transfiguring the imagination of masses of ignorant men.
(D) W. Lewis, British official in Champaran, report, (1917)

The result was a foregone conclusion. Gandhi proved his case. The question of indemnifying the peasants arose, and the commission recommended a 25 per cent refund of the illegal exactions. When he was asked why he had not held out for a full 100 per cent, he replied that by making the planters pay back a quarter of the money they had stolen from the tenants, he had destroyed their prestige.
(E) Robert Payne, 'Mahatma Gandhi', (1969)

Gandhi's revolutionary significance lay in his attempt to release the energies contained in the endurance of the Indian people. This he sought to do by his complete identification with the average Indian. It was from his strong sense of unity with the starving, naked and ignorant masses of India that he derived his own power.
(F) Humayun Kabir, 'The Visva-Bharati Quarterly', (1949)

Mr Gandhi does not wish to hurt the propertied class. He is even opposed to a campaign against them. He has no passion for economic equality. Referring to the propertied class Mr Gandhi said quite recently that he does not wish to destroy the hen that lays the golden egg.
(G) B.R. Ambedkar, 'What Congress and Gandhi Have Done to the Untouchables', (1946)

Gandhi, who was deeply concerned by peasant problems, won over the existing peasant organisations. It was a kind of paradox for him to do so, for Congress was getting its financial support and administrative direction from the middle classes, who were likely to be landowners. Gandhi's own attitude was that... all should unselfishly work together... Under the application of this teaching the landlords lost nothing and the peasants gained nothing.
(H) Norman Brown, 'The United States and India', (1953)

see pages 35-37

1. *How do sources A and B help to explain why Gandhi travelled in Champaran by the means illustrated in source C?*

2. *Employ sources in this unit to explain why British officials would be making reports on Gandhi's activities in Champaran.*

3. *What reason is given in source E for Gandhi accepting only a partial refund for illegal exaction? What explanation is implied in sources G and H?*

Unit 6: Campaigns 1920-1922

The next year (1920) the Congress took the plunge, and adopted Gandhi's programme of non-cooperation... The method of struggle was a perfectly peaceful one, non-violent as it was called, and the basis was a refusal to help the government in its administration and exploitation of India... this programme was a totally different thing from what the Congress had so far been doing.
(A) Jawaharlal Nehru, 'Toward Freedom', (1941)

You may hang us on the gallows, you may send us to prison, but you will get no cooperation from us. You will get it in jail or on the gallows, but not in the regiments of the army... This Empire has been guilty of such terrible atrocities that... it was the duty of every Indian to destroy it.
(B) Gandhi, speech, (1920)

A demonstration was passing the police barracks; the police jeered at the crowd and a few shots were fired. Thereupon the crowd set fire to the police barracks and many policemen were killed. Instantly, Gandhi called off the whole movement of civil disobedience... His politically minded colleagues were furious. Over months and years, the great revolution had been prepared. Here, just because of an isolated act of violence, the whole thing was thrown away and India was left in dismay... To (Gandhi) it was better that the British system, much as he now hated it, should continue for years rather than that it should be overthrown by violence.
(C) H. Alexander, 'Gandhi Through Western Eyes', (1969)

To sound the order of retreat just when public enthusiasm was reaching the boiling point was nothing short of a national calamity. The principle lieutenants of the Mahatma, ... who were all in prison, shared the popular resentment. I was with the Deshbandhu at the time, and I could see that he was beside himself with anger and sorrow.
(D) Subhas Bose, The Indian Struggle, (1935)

It is impossible for me to disassociate myself from the diabolical crimes of Chauri Chata or the mad outrages of Bombay. He (prosecuting counsel) is quite right when he says that as a man of responsibility, as a man having a fair share of education, having a fair share of experience of this world, I should have known the consequences of every one of my acts. I knew that I was playing with fire...I want to avoid violence. Non-violence is the first article of my faith... I know that my people have sometimes gone mad. I am deeply sorry for it, and I am, therefore, here ... to invite and cheerfully submit to the highest penalty that can be inflicted upon me.
(E) Gandhi, speech to the court, (March, 1922)

By the end of December all the best-known Congress leaders, except Gandhi were imprisoned. Twenty thousand political prisoners filled the jails. At the highest point of the struggle, at the beginning of the following year, 30,000 were in jail. Enthusiasm was at fever heat... Gandhi was now Dictator of the Congress... Full powers had been placed in his hands to lead it to victory. The movement had come to the final trial of strength, for the launching of mass civil disobedience. The whole country was looking to Gandhi. What would he do?... At a hasty meeting of the Working Committee at Bardoli on February 12, the decision was reached, in view of the "inhuman conduct of the mob at Chauri Chaura," to end, not only mass civil disobedience, but the whole campaign of civil disobedience through volunteer processions, the holding of public meetings under ban and the like, and to substitute a "constructive" programme of spinning, temperance reform and educational activities. The battle was over. The mountain had indeed borne a mouse.
(F) Rajani Palme Dutt, 'India Today', (1949)

Gandhi, the politician, hopelessly blundered. He sounded the order of retreat just when the public enthusiasm had reached its boiling point... Judged by all rational standards, Gandhi committed a great tactical blunder, leading to deplorable consequences in the political situation in India.
(G) R.Majumdar, 'History of the Freedom Movement', (1963)

He gave us a scare! His programme filled our jails. You can't go on arresting people forever you know - not when there are 319,000,000 of them. And if they had taken the next step and refused to pay taxes! God knows where we should have been. Gandhi's was the most colossal experiment in world history; and it came within an inch of succeeding. But he couldn't control men's passions. They became violent and he called off his programme. You know the rest. We jailed him.
(H) Lord Lloyd, Governor of Bombay, Interview, (1939)

He valued the individual and believed that the freedom of the individual could be attained only through the discipline of non-violence. In mob frenzy the individual surrenders his independence. The incursion of mob frenzy into political action meant for Gandhi the end of the struggle.
(I) Humayun Kabir, 'The Visva-Bharati Quarterly', (1949)

see pages 39-41

1. Select passages from sources C, D, F, G and I that reveal whether the historian is hostile or sympathetic to Gandhi's decision to call-off his non-cooperation campaign.

2. How would an historian hostile to Gandhi's decision in 1922 use source H to help support his point of view?

3. Comment on the change in Gandhi's tone in sources B and E.

INDIA
is the World's Greatest
Buyer of British Goods

Last year India and Burma spent more than £85,000,000 on imports from this country. Think what that means in wages. Think of the employment these huge Indian orders give. Think how the prosperity of our own great textile industries, our iron and steel and machinery and engineering works depend on the prosperity of your fellow-citizens in India.

Is not that a convincing reason for buying Indian produce in return?

It is by buying from India and from the whole Empire—butter and fruit from Australia, apples and cheese from Canada, mutton and lamb from New Zealand, wine and tobacco from South Africa—that we enrich our friends and our friends enrich us.

INDIA sends us	
Tea	Coffee
Rice	Tobacco
Wheat & Barley	
Lentils	Pepper
Curries	Spices
and Chutneys	

(A) Advertisement in 'The Times', (1926)

It is not the British people who rule India, but modern civilisation rules India through its railways, telegraph, telephone, etc... If British rule were replaced tomorrow by Indian rule based on modern methods, India would be none the better, except that she would be able then to retain some of the money which is drained away to England... India's salvation consists in unlearning what she has learnt during the past fifty years. The railways, telegraphs, hospitals, lawyers, doctors and such will have to go.

(B) Gandhi, 'Confession of Faith', (1909)

He (Gandhi) had inherited from the early Congress its ideal of 'swadeshi' (economic self-reliance)... Gandhi, however, significantly altered the content of 'swadeshi', with its championing of Indian manufactures over imported, especially British, products. His was a vision of self-sufficiency.

(C) Antony Copley, 'Gandhi', (1987)

Modern civilisation must be unlearned, the factories must be torn down, the hospitals must be abandoned, the railroad tracks must be torn up, the great cities must be swept away, and men should live in close proximity to the soil, with simple plows and wearing hand-spun garments, labouring to earn their daily bread... All this was, of course, in the highest degree reactionary, for Gandhi permitted no change in the relationship between the feudal lord and his peasant servants, the rich and the poor.

(D) Robert Payne, 'Mahatma Gandhi', (1969)

Machinery in the past has made us dependent on England, and the only way we can rid ourselves of that dependence is to boycott all goods made by machinery. That is why we have made it the patriotic duty of every Indian to spin his own cotton and weave his own cloth. This is our form of attacking a very powerful nation like England.

(E) Gandhi, in conversation with Charlie Chaplin, (1931)

Leisure means the lessening of the toil and effort necessary for satisfying the physical wants of life. How can leisure be made possible?... Only when machine takes the place of man... Machinery and modern civilisation are thus indispensable for emancipating man from leading the life of a brute... In short, Gandhism with its call of back to nature, means back to nakedness, back to squalor, back to poverty and back to ignorance for the vast mass of the people.

(F) B.R. Ambedkar, 'The Congress and Gandhi', (1946)

1. *Describe how Gandhi changed the 'swadeshi' campaign.*

2. *How does source A help to explain the last sentence in source E?*

3. *Identify and explain the source in this unit which agrees with Robert Payne's comment that Gandhi's swadeshi campaign was "reactionary".*

Unit 8:   The Salt March

In a hot climate salt is almost a necessity for man and beast. The Hindu of past ages could pan his own, or pick it up out of natural deposits... Under the British Raj the only legal salt was government salt from guarded depots. The price had a built-in levy... Yet eastward, westward and southward, at the end of all the sacred rivers, lay the open acres of God's salt water.

(A) Geoffrey Ashe, 'Gandhi', (1968)

Take your own salary... You are getting much over five thousand times India's average income... The whole revenue system has to be revised as to make the peasant's good its primary concern. But the British system seems to be designed to crush the very life out of him. Even the salt he must use to live is so taxed as to make the burden fall heaviest on him.

(B) Gandhi, letter to Lord Irwin, (2, March, 1930)

Gandhi had thought long about the nature of the first act of civil disobedience. He had learned that, to rouse the masses, it was necessary to use some symbol they could easily recognise. There was no point in slogans about dominion status, because the masses had no idea of what that was. Gandhi hit upon the salt tax... Gandhi reached the sea, ceremonially made his uneatable salt - and broke the law... On the same day, salt was made at about five thousand meetings throughout India; Congress gave five million as the official number of those involved, but anything in India can draw a crowd and it is certain that the majority of those who attended the ceremonies did so as casual onlookers.

(C) M. Edwardes, 'The Last Years of British India', (1963)

With an unerring instinct for a simple and at the same time dramatic effect, Gandhi chose to inaugurate his satyagrapha campaign with a march to the sea at Dandi... (Gandhi) reached Dandi on 5th April after marching 241 miles in 24 days, broke the salt laws and sparked off a nationwide movement for similar defiance of authority.

(D) Durga Das, 'India', (1969)

2,500 marchers, armed only with ropes to pull down the barbed wire stockade of the salt works and committed to using no violence, waded through ditches surrounding the stockade and advanced in silent columns. The police charged with steel laths to whack the unprotected skulls of the marchers. The leaders of the march were arrested and over three hundred were treated in a makeshift hospital. Two died... Indians had publically displayed what had been their fate for ages past: the capacity to accept suffering.

(E) William Golant, 'The Long Afternoon', (1975)

They marched steadily with heads up, without the encouragement of music or cheering or any possibility that they might escape serious injury or death. The police rushed out and methodically and mechanically beat down the second column. There was no fight, nor struggle; the marchers simply walked forward until struck down. There were no outcries, only groans after they fell... Not one of the marchers even raised an arm to fend off the blows.
(F) Webb Miller, American journalist at Dandi, (1930)

Your Majesty can hardly fail to have read with amusement the accounts of several battles for the Salt Depot at Dharasana. The police for a long time tried to refrain from action. After a time this became impossible, and they eventually had to resort to sterner measures. A good many people suffered minor injuries in consequence, but I believe those who suffered injuries were as nothing compared with those who wished to sustain an honourable contusion or bruise, or who, to make the whole setting more dramatic, lay on the ground as if laid out for dead without any injury at all. But of course, as Your Majesty will appreciate, the whole business was propaganda and, as such, served its purpose admirably well.
(G) Lord Irwin, letter to King George V, (April, 1930)

What has become of English honour, English justice? No amount of argument can excuse what they have been doing at Dharasana. India has now realised the true nature of the British Raj, and with this realisation the Raj is doomed.
(H) Madeleine Slade, eyewitness at Dandi, letter, (1930)

Those who live in England, far away from the East, have now got to realise that Europe has completely lost her former prestige in Asia. She is no longer regarded as the champion throughout the world of fair dealing and the exponent of high principle, but the upholder of race supremacy and the exploiter of those outside her borders... For Europe this is, in actual fact, a great moral defeat that has happened... (Asia) can now afford to look down on Europe where before she looked up.
(I) Rabindranath Tagore, interview in 'The Guardian', (1930)

see pages 42-44

1. *Select passages from at least three sources in this unit to show why Gandhi decided to organise the salt march to Dandi.*

2. *Compare sources C and D's interpretation of the masses reaction to Gandhi's actions in Dandi. Give reasons for this difference in interpretation.*

3. *Give as many reasons as you can why Lord Irwin would have been more concerned by the presence at Dandi of Webb Miller than Madeleine Slade.*

Unit 9: Round Table Conference

A Round Table Conference was held in London in 1930. Congress refused to attend. Representatives of the princes attended and, what was more, agreed to enter a future Indian federation. This was a tempting bait for Congress. Gandhi was released from prison and had a series of meetings with Lord Irwin. This was a strange conjunction and prelude to many other such meetings: the aristocratic leader of a declining empire wooing the nationalist rebel. After prolonged and characteristically intricate discussion, Gandhi agreed to attend a second session of the Round Table.

(A) A.J.P. Taylor, 'English History 1914-1945', (1965)

I suppose the real difficulty is an utter lack of courage, moral and political, among the natives, no individual dare take an independent line of his own, and this really shows how unfit they are for anything like self-government.

(B) King George V, letter to Lord Irwin, (1928)

(C) "Simplicissimus', German magazine, (1931)

76

Amid a flurry of speculation as to what he would wear, Gandhi went to tea with George V and Queen Mary. He was dressed as usual. The King made solemn remarks about the wrongness of subverting 'my Empire', which Gandhi tactfully turned aside. When the ordeal was over, somebody asked him if he really thought he had enough clothes on. 'It was quite all right,' he said; 'the King had enough on for both of us.'

(D) Geoffrey Ashe, 'Gandhi', (1968)

It was arranged that at the party I was to fetch up Gandhi at a suitable moment for presentation to the King. When the time came, Gandhi's Khaddar made it easy for me to find him amongst the black coats and ceremonial clothes of the delegates. When I presented him, there was a difficult moment. The King was obviously thinking of Gandhi's responsibility for civil disobedience. However, when they were once started, the King's simple sincerity and Gandhi's beautiful manners combined to smooth the course of the conversation, though more than once I became nervous when the King looked resentfully at Gandhi's knees... Just as Gandhi was taking his leave, His Majesty could not refrain from uttering a grave warning. 'Remember, Mr Gandhi, I won't have any attacks on my Empire.' I held by breath in fear of an argument between the two. Gandhi saved the situation with a grave and deferential reply, 'I must not be drawn into a political argument in Your Majesty's Palace after receiving your Majesty's hospitality.' They then took leave of each other as friendly guest and host. A very honest King and a great diplomat, I thought to myself.

(E) Lord Templewood, Secretary of State for India, (1931)

His Majesty was, as is his custom, very nice to Gandhi... but ended up by impressing on him that this country would not stand a campaign of terrorism and having their friends shot down in India. His Majesty warned Gandhi that he was to put a stop to this... Gandhi spluttered some excuse, but His Majesty said he was responsible.

(F) Sir Clive Wigram, the King's Private Secretary, letter to the Viceroy of India, (1930)

see pages 46-48

1. *What do the sources in this unit tell us about King George's views on the Indian Independence Movement?*

2. *Compare sources E and F's interpretation of Gandhi's meeting with George V. Both these men were present when the incident took place. Can you explain why they have different recollections of the incident?*

3. *Explain the meaning of source C.*

Unit 10: Gandhi's Personality

While he was prepared to go all out for the causes which he championed, he never forgot the human background of the situation, never lost his temper or succumbed to hate, and preserved his gentle humour even in the most trying conditions.
(A) Jan Smuts, 'Reflections on Gandhi', (1939)

He (Gandhi) had great faith in vows, and no doubt they often strengthened his will in undertaking enterprises and standing firm in the face of trials... The vow of non-stealing was so interpreted as to mean that no member ought to possess anything he could fairly live without. If he kept things he did not really need, he was a thief.
(B) H. Alexander, 'Gandhi Through Western Eyes', (1969)

I have seen the whole course of his life changed in a few moments in obedience to an inner call from God which comes to him in silent prayer. ...(Gandhi's) faith in God will never allow him to yield to man.
(C) Charlie Andrews, 'A Tribute to a Friend', (1939)

In matters of conscience I am uncompromising. Nobody can make me yield. I, therefore, tolerate the charge of being a dictator.
(D) Gandhi, 'Navajivan', (January, 1921)

This voice (Gandhi's)... was quiet and low, and yet it could be heard above the shouting of the multitude; it was soft and gentle, and yet there seemed to be steel hidden away somewhere in it; it was courteous and full of appeal, and yet there was something grim and frightening in it... Behind the language of peace and friendship there was power and the quivering shadow of action and a determination not to submit to a wrong.
(E) Jawaharlal Nehru, 'Toward Freedom', (1941)

Another saintly feature we discern in him is the absence of any trace of egotism. He was very much embarrassed when he was called a saint. He gave strict instructions to the inmates of his ashram that he should be referred to only as Gandhiji and not as Mahatma Gandhi. When he heard the report that in some place a temple had been built and his idol installed, he grew very angry and said it was an insult to him and asked the organisers to remove the idol and use the building as a spinning centre.
(F) D.S. Sarma, 'The Father of the Nation', (1956)

Generations to come, it may be, will scarce believe that such a one as this ever in flesh and blood walked upon this earth.
(G) Albert Einstein, statement, (1948)

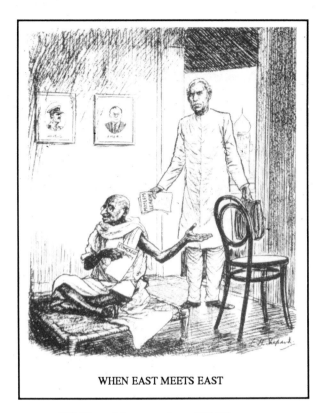

WHEN EAST MEETS EAST

(H) 'Punch' magazine, (1944)

No one without his personality and saintly character would have inspired that confidence and created the will and enthusiasm which alone could galvanise the masses into action. The saint had always had a profound appeal to the Indian mind. It is the great credit of Gandhi - perhaps unique in the world's history - that he could exploit the spirit of devotion and complete self-surrender, usually reserved for a spiritual 'Guru', for political purposes.

(I) R. Majumdar, 'History of the Freedom Movement in India', (1963)

1. *What would you want to know about the authors of these sources before making a judgement about their importance and accuracy?*

2. *What is source H saying about Gandhi? Which sources in this unit support this point of view?*

3. *Give an overall view of Gandhi's personality based on the sources in this unit.*

Unit 11: Quit India Campaign

The Indian Army expanded from 189,000 in 1939 to 2,500,000 in 1945; at the same time, a force of eight million men were employed for special tasks required by the defence services, five million in war industries and an extra million to meet the strain on the railways
(A) Philip Mason, 'A Matter of Honour', (1974)

Economic and strategic factors led to Japanese expansion into South-East Asia: Malaya would provide rubber and tea, the East Indies oil, bauxite and rubber... but Japan saw no advantage in 1942 in pressing on with any attempted invasion of India.
(B) Antony Copley, 'Gandhi', (1987)

I am engaged here in meeting by far the most serious rebellion since that of 1857, the gravity and extent of which we have so far concealed from the world for reasons of military security.
(C) Lord Linlithgow, Viceroy of India, letter, (1942)

The cry of 'Quit India' has arisen from a realisation of the fact that if India is to shoulder the burden of representing or fighting for the cause of mankind, she must have the glow of freedom now. Has a freezing man ever been warmed by the promise of the warmth of the sunshine coming at some future date?... If the British wish to document their right to win the war and make the world better, they must purify themselves by surrendering power in India... We are asked to fight for democracy in Germany, Italy and Japan. How can we when we haven't got it ourselves?... I do not want Japan to win. I do not want the Axis to win... But I am sure that Britain cannot win unless the Indian people become free. Britain is weaker and Britain is morally indefensible while she rules India.
(D) Gandhi, interview with Louis Fischer, (June, 1942)

I believe all war to be wholly wrong. But if we scrutinize the motives of two warring parties, we may find one to be in the right and the other in the wrong. For instance, if A wishes to seize B's country, B is obviously the wronged one. Both fight with arms. I do not believe in violent warfare but all the same B, whose cause is just, deserves my moral help and blessings.
(E) Gandhi, 'Harijan', (August 18, 1940)

On one occasion in Patna City a number of women laid themselves down on the ground right across the street and held up all the traffic. When the Superintendent of Police arrived on the scene he was at first nonplussed. If they had been men he would have sent in policemen to lift them out bodily, but he daren't do it with women. So he thought for a bit and then he called for fire hoses and with the hoses they sprayed these women who were lying on the ground. They only wore very thin saris and, of course, when the water got on them all their figures could be seen. The constables started cracking dirty jokes and immediately the women got up and ran.

(F) F.C. Hart, Indian Special Branch, Interview, (1975)

Tokyo radio... announced that the armies of Nippon were coming to free India from British tyranny... In August (1942), the All-India Congress Committee declared a 'mass struggle' to force Britain to quit India... the next day, (Gandhi) and the whole working committee, as well as a number of other Congress leaders, were quietly arrested... Congress was once again declared illegal and the British set about suppressing what appeared to be a full-scale rebellion. Extreme nationalists indulged in extensive sabotage... By the middle of September, 250 railway stations had been destroyed or seriously damaged.

(G) M. Edwardes, 'The Last Years of British India', (1963)

Bose urged Congress to launch a national revolution to overthrow British rule when war broke out in September. His speeches to this effect, which led to his arrest in 1940, failed to move the Congress leadership. It was at this point that Bose decided to seek foreign support in the liberation of India. Following his escape from India, Bose spent two years in Berlin. He was under no illusions about his hosts but turned a blind eye to the excesses to the Nazi regime: "My enemy's enemy is my friend" became his motto... To lead an Indian army in the liberation of his country was now Bose's greatest ambition. At Singapore he inherited the remnants of the Indian National Army (INA) which the Japanese had formed in 1942 from deserters and prisoners-of-war.

(H) Stephen Ashton, 'Indian Independence', (1985)

see pages 48-51

1. *Durga Das has claimed that the Second World War more than anything else in history, "hastened the liquidation of the British Raj in India." How do sources D, G and H help to explain this statement.*

2. *Why was it necessary for the Viceroy of India to hide the full facts of the 'Quit India' campaign?*

4. *With reference to source F, explain the usefulness to the historian of interviews with participants in past events.*

Unit 12: The Caste System

A man could not rise from the class he was born in, nor could a high-class man marry, take food from, or otherwise socially mix with, one of a lower class without being ritually polluted. Those outside the Hindu system were (the) untouchables, who performed menial or degrading tasks... Christians and Muslims, no matter how exalted they might be in rank and power, were also outcaste, ritually unclean, and so avoided by respectable Hindus as far as possible outside official duties.

(A) T.A. Heathcote, 'The Indian Army', (1975)

Gandhi did not attack, or ask for the liquidation of, the Hindu system of caste as the supreme barrier between the Hindus and the Muslims. The fundamental assumption of Hindu social organisation is that a man is born - must be born - in one of the four castes and must remain in it and die in it. None can enter the fold; none can get out of it.

(B) K. Sarwar Hasan, 'The Genesis of Pakistan', (1950)

To destroy the caste system and adopt Western European social system means that Hindus must give up the principle of hereditary occupation which is the soul of the caste system... To change it is to create disorder... I am opposed to all those who are out to destroy the caste system.

(C) Gandhi, 'Nava-Jivan', (1921)

UNITED INDIA.

(D) David Low, 'London Evening Standard', (1928)

(Gandhi) stated that caste was essential for the best possible adjustment of social stability and progress, but he warned that it must not connote superiority or inferiority...the Untouchables constituted nearly forty million people; they were denied even the ordinary facilities of life...In the name of Hinduism and in the name of an independent and prosperous India he appealed to everyone to erase the curse of Untouchability. He (Gandhi) addressed meetings from one end of India to the other, denouncing the degeneration it had brought with it. He fasted, fully prepared to sacrifice even his life for the "noble cause of removal of Untouchability."

(D) T. Unnithan, 'Gandhi and Free India', (1956)

The Hindu sacred law penalised the 'Shudras' (Hindus of the fourth class) from acquiring wealth. It is a law of enforced poverty unknown in any other part of the world. What does Gandhism do? It does not lift the ban. It blesses the 'Shudra' for the moral courage to give up property...Mr Gandhi has most categorically stated that removal of Untouchability does not mean inter-dining or inter-marriage between the Hindus and the Untouchables. Mr Gandhi's anti-Untouchability means that the Untouchables will be classed as 'Shudras' instead of being classed as 'Atishudras'... Will they have the right to choose their profession? Can they adopt the career of lawyer, doctor or engineer? To these questions the answer which Gandhism gives is an emphatic "no". The Untouchables must follow their hereditary professions.

(E) B.R. Ambedkar, 'What Congress and Gandhi Have Done to the Untouchables', (1946)

An organisation headed and symbolised by Gandhi was necessarily an emotional, semi-religious appeal to the Hindu masses and not to the Muslims; for Gandhi with all his fads and fastings, his goat's milk, mud baths, days of silence and fetish of non-violence was pre-eminently a Hindu. He himself claimed to be "a Muslim, a Hindu, a Buddhist, a Christian, a Jew, a Parsee." But this claim did not cut much ice; indeed who but a Hindu could entertain such a preposterous hope of being all things to all men?

(F) Penderel Moon, 'Divide and Quit', (1961)

see pages 34-35

1. *"Gandhi disapproved of the caste system." Is this statement supported by the sources in this unit?*
2. *Explain the meaning of source D. Compare the views being expressed by David Low with those by K. Sarwar Hasan and Penderel Moon.*
3. *Which sources in this unit are written by: (a) a muslim; (b) an untouchable; and (c) a supporter of the Congress Party?*

Unit 13: Partition

The two separate communities lived uneasily together. Under British rule the two religions had separate electorates, education, press, literature and languages, which contributed to an aggressive and uncompromising attitude towards the other community... Though Hindus outnumbered Muslims by about three to one over all of India, in some areas, Bengal, the North-West Frontier, Baluchistan, and the Punjab, the majority of the population were Muslims.

(A) William Golant,'The Long Afternoon', (1975)

The reason commonly given in England for refusing the demand for Indian self-government was that it would only lead to violent conflict and civil war all over India... the British must remain to keep peace as far as possible. When I first visited India in 1927, I was startled to find British officials who quite openly said: "So long as we keep the Hindus and Muslims in conflict, our Government will not be in danger."

(B) H. Alexander, 'Gandhi Through Western Eyes', (1969)

Before the British came to India, there seems to have been little hostility between Hindus and Muslims; everywhere they seem to have lived together for the most part peacefully and harmoniously... The British policy in India has been from the beginning that known as "divide and rule,"... This has been the policy of all great conquerors and rulers of foreign peoples, from those of ancient Babylonia, Assyria, Persia and Egypt down to Napoleon in Europe and Clive in India... Indeed without employing this policy of stirring up hostility... the British could never have conquered the land... knowing well that divisions always weaken a nation and render it easier to hold in subjection.

(C) Jabez Sunderland, 'India in Bondage', (1960)

It is the old maxim of 'divide and rule'. But there is a division of labour here. We divide and you rule.

(D) Muslim leader, interview, (1931)

The fearful massacres, which are occurring in India, are no surprise to me. We are, of course, only at the beginning of these horrors and butcheries, perpetrated upon one another with the ferocity of cannibals by the races gifted with the capacities for the highest culture and who had for generations dwelt side by side in general peace under the broad, tolerant and impartial rule of the British Crown and Parliament.

(E) Winston Churchill, speech, (September, 1947)

	Hindus	Muslims	Sikhs
Bengal	21,570,407	27,497,624	10
Punjab	6,328,588	13,332,624	3,064,144
North-West Frontier	142,977	2,227,303	42,510
Baluchistan	41,432	405,309	3,368

(F) Population of four provinces, (1931)

An orgy of killing in Calcutta was followed by communal riots on a large scale in some other parts of India. This had the expected impact... and the British Government announced that no constitution would be imposed upon any unwilling parts of the country. In other words, the only problem now, as far as the British were concerned, was to decide which areas should constitute Pakistan. The Congress also, with some bitterness, came around to accepting what now seemed inevitable. Gandhi alone still held out. He was willing even that the British should remain in India rather than leave after dividing the country... But the other leaders of the Congress did not regard the unity of India as the supreme value. They were tired and ageing men who wished, in the evening of their lives, to hold the levers of authority.

(G) S. Gopal, 'Modern India', (1967)

All his life Gandhi had dreamed of an India at peace, bringing peace to the world by example... He had dreamed of bringing into existence a new India free of foreign domination and dedicated to 'ahimsa', the Muslims and Hindus living quietly side by side... Now, at the very moment when freedom was being wrested from the British, the dream of a peaceful India was shattered.

(H) Robert Payne, Mahatma Gandhi, (1969)

see pages 51-53

1. Which source in this unit provides evidence to support the views expressed in source A?

2. Select passages from the sources in this unit to help explain the policy of 'divide and rule'.

3. Which source takes the view that Britain helped to keep the peace in India. Explain this view.

4. What was Gandhi's opinion on Partition? How did this viewpoint differ from other leaders of the Congress Party?

Unit 14: Assassination of Gandhi

Death is the appointed end of all life. To die by the hand of a brother rather than by disease or in some other way cannot be for me a matter of sorrow. And if even in such a case I am free from the thoughts of anger or hatred against my assailant,
(A) Gandhi in conversation with General Smuts, (1908)

If I should die of a lingering disease, or even from a pimple, then you must shout from the housetops to the whole world that I was a false Mahatma. ... If I die of an illness, you must declare me to be a false or hypocritical Mahatma, even at the risk of people cursing you... if someone shot at me and I received his bullet in my bare chest without a sigh and with Rama's name on my lips, only then should you say that I was a true Mahatma.
(B) Gandhi talking to Manubehn, (January 29, 1948)

Suddenly a man in a khaki jacket pushed through from the right. It was the conspirator Godse. Manu thought he was a pilgrim prostrating himself in the Mahatma's path, and as they were late, she put out a hand to check him. He thrust her away so hard that she stumbled. Two feet from Gandhi he actually did make a brief bow. Then he raised a pistol and fired three shots. The first bullet entered Gandhi's abdomen and came out through his back. It caught him in mid-stride... The second passed between his ribs and also came out the back. A bloodstain appeared on his white shawl. His hands sank. The third bullet struck his chest above the right nipple and lodged in the lung. His face turned grey... In these last instants, bystanders heard him gasping the divine name Rama.
(C) Geoffrey Ashe, 'Gandhi', (1968)

Round spectacles and false teeth. Worn sandals. A portable spinning wheel. A slim, well-thumbed copy of the 'Bhagavad Gita', a Hindu scripture. Two bowls. A pen and a letter opener. Three small make-believe monkeys... A dollar watch. A spittoon. These were all the wordly possessions of Mohandas Karamchand Gandhi, the Mahatma, or "great soul," when a Hindu fanatic assassinated him on January 30, 1948.
(D) Paul Grimes, 'Soul Force', (1979)

GANDHI IS KILLED BY A HINDU; INDIA SHAKEN; WORLD MOURNS; 15 DIE IN RIOTING IN BOMBAY

NEW DELHI - Mohandas K. Gandhi was killed by an assassin's bullet today. The assassin was a Hindu who fired three shots from a pistol at a range of three feet. The 78-year-old Gandhi, who was the one person who held discordant elements together and kept some sort of unity in this turbulent land, was shot down at 5:15 pm as he was proceeding through the Birla House gardens to the pergola from which he was to deliver his daily prayer meeting.

(E) 'New York Times', (January, 31, 1948)

The accumulating provocation of thirty-two years, culminating in the last pro-Muslim fast, at last goaded me to the conclusion that the existence of Gandhi should be brought to an end immediately... I felt that the Indian politics in the absence of Gandhi would surely be practical, able to retaliate, and would be powerful with armed forces. No doubt, my own future would be totally ruined, but the nation would be saved from the inroads of Pakistan... I declare before man and God that in putting an end to Gandhi's life I have removed one who was a curse to India, a force for evil, and who had, during thirty years of egotistic pursuit of hare-brained policy, brought nothing but misery and unhappiness... I do not think that the Nehru government will understand me, but I have little doubt that history will give me justice and I am content with that prospect.

(F) Nathuram Godse, speech in court, (May, 1948)

see pages 55-56

1. *What evidence is there in this unit that Gandhi predicted his own death? How accurate was this prediction?*

2. *Geoffrey Ashe did not witness Gandhi's assassination but in source C he gives a detailed account of the incident. What sources would Ashe have needed to consult before he wrote this account?*

3. *Study the headline and opening paragraph of the New York Times report on Gandhi's death. With reference to source E, explain the function of headlines in newspapers.*

4. *Explain why Godse killed Gandhi. Was Godse right when he said that "history will give me justice"?*

Coursework Assignments

It is 1944. As a member of MI5 you have been asked to investigate Gandhi's political activities. You have been instructed to take an especially close look at the claim that Gandhi is a 'Bolshevik agitator'. Write a report on your findings.

You should find the following sources helpful:

Unit 2: B, C and F; Unit 5: B; Unit 6: B; Unit 8: B,C and D; Unit 9: D, E and F; Unit 11: D, F, G and H.

Write a letter to a newspaper claiming that Gandhi was (i) a pacifist who inspired the modern peace movement or (ii) a political activist who only used non-violence as a strategy when it suited his objectives.

You should find the following sources helpful:

Unit 2: G; Unit 3: A, B, C, D, F and G; Unit 4: A, B, C and D; Unit 6: A, C, E, F, H and I; Unit 8: E; Unit 11: D; Unit 13: G and H.

Write an obituary for Gandhi that might have appeared in his own newspaper, 'Harijan', on January 31st, 1948.

Bibliography

Alexander, H.	Gandhi Through Western Eyes	Asia, 1969
Allen, C.	Plain Tales from the Raj	Andre Deutsch, 1975
Allen, C.	A Scrapbook of British India	Andre Deutsch, 1975
Ambedkar, B.	What Congress and Gandhi have Done to the Untouchables	Thacker, Bombay, 1946
Andrews, M.	Mahatma Gandhi's Ideas	George Allen & Unwin, 1929
Ashe, G.	Gandhi	Stein & Day, 1968
Ashton, S.	Indian Independence	Batsford, 1985
Bose, C.	The Indian Struggle 1920-1934	Wishart, 1935
Brown, W.	The United States and India	Harvard Press, 1953
Chakrabarti, A.	The Lonesome Pilgrim	Allied, Bombay, 1969
Copley, A.	Gandhi	Basil Blackwell, 1987
Das, D.	India	Collins, 1969
Dutt, P	India Today	Bombay, 1949
Edwardes, M.	The Last Years of British India	Cassell, 1963
Fischer, L.	Gandhi: His Life and Message	Mentor, 1954
Fischer, L. (ed.)	The Essential Gandhi	George Allen & Unwin, 1963
Gandhi, M.	Hind Swarf	Navajivan, 1909
Gandhi, M.	An Autobiography	Navajivan, 1927
Golant, W.	The Long Afternoon	Purnell, 1975
Gopal, S.	Modern India	Historical Association, 1967
Hasan. K.	The Genesis of Freedom	Karachi, 1950
Heathcote, T.	The Indian Army	David & Charles, 1974
Kabir, H	Gandhiji and the Indian Revolution	Visa-Bharati Quarterly, 1949
Lewis, M. (ed.)	Gandhi: Maker of Modern India	Heath, 1965
Majumdar, R	Three Phases of India's Struggle	Bharatiya, Calcutta, 1961
Majumdar, R.	History of the Freedom Movement in India	Bharatiya, Calcutta, 1963
Mason, P.	A Matter of Honour	Purnell, 1974
Mason, P.	The Men Who Ruled India	Jonathan Cape, 1985
Menrotra, S.	Gandhi and the Commonwealth	India Quarterly, 1961
Menon, V.	The Transfer of Power	Princeton University, 1957
Moon, P.	Divide and Quit	Chatto & Windus, 1961
Nehru, J.	Toward Freedom	Bodley Head, 1939
Nehru, J.	Glimpses of World History	John Day, 1942
Nehru, J.	India and the World	George Allen & Allen, 1936
Panikkar, K.	The Foundations of New India	George Allen & Unwin, 1963
Pandit, V.	The Scope of Happiness	Weidenfeld & Nicolson, 1979
Payne, R.	The Life and Death of Gandhi	Bodley Head, 1969
Radhakrishnan, S.	Mahatma Gandhi: 100 Years	Gandhi Foundation, 1968

Rawding, F.	Gandhi	Cambridge, 1980
Rothermund, I.	Gandhi's Strategy	Prakashan, Bombay, 1963
Sarma, D.	The Father of the Nation	Madras, 1956
Savarkar, V.	Hindu Rashtra Darshan	Bombay, 1949
Sunderland, T.	India in Bondage	Lewis Copland, 1960
Unnithan, T.	Gandhi and Free India	Groningen, 1956
Wallbank, T. (ed.)	The Partition of India,	Heath, 1966